from the

~~Out~~ Farmhouse

to the

Green ~~Pent~~house

from the Outhouse *to the* Greenhouse
Copyright © 2018 by Brianna Walker

All rights reserved. No part of this book may be reproduced in any form by any electronic or mechanical means including photocopying, recording, or information storage and retrieval without permission in writing from the author.

ISBN-13:
978-1719094689

ISBN-10:
1719094683

Give feedback on the book at:
farmersfate@agritimesnw.com

Printed in U.S.A

Dedicated To:
K & P
who hold my whole heart

The Fun

Abstinence Prevents Minivans 11
Dr. Pendyke's Miracle Salve 13
Kids, Parties & Toothbrushes 17
Farm Hair, Don't Care 20
Hieroglyphic English 23
Fitbits and *Fat*bits 26
Curious Parker & The Man in the Yellow Hat 28
Conned with the Truth 31
Surfing the 50-50-90 Rule 34
Passport Photo Resemblance 38
You Know You're From a Small Town When 41
Boys and Their Dogs 43
My Uncle's Uterus 46
Calendars, Storks & Redneck Labor 50
All Ya Gotta Do is Act Naturally 53
ArgueNaked 56
Spring Diet Duet 59
Sardines and Baked Beans 61
Forgotten Father's Day 64
Joe's Buffalo 66
Do Something Sexy to a Tractor 69
The House that Peter-Bilt 72

The Frustration

Word Processors and Funerals..77
Carrots, Eggs & Dead Crabs..80
Fifty Shades of Hay...83
Save a Horse, Ride a Tractor..86
The Toilet Paper Stay-cation...89
Do You Wanna Build a Snowman...92
The Sands of Time..95
Jim's Drops of Kindness..98
His Version, My Version..101
Grandpa's Ivy League Education...104
Wiped Out...111
Raining on the Wicked Witch...114
Up a Creek with Half a Paddle..117
I've Got Ewe Babe...Me & Ewe..120
Racing Through VBS...123
It's a Ladder Kind of Days...126

The Funny Smells

The Little Half Moon...133
Men & Their Crazy "Two Canoe" Ideas...136
Pete the Parrot...139
Pink Pants, Invisible Clothes and the Truth...................................142
The 8th Day of the Week..145
The Flat Out Truth..147
What's in Your Lunchbox?..150
When I Said "I Do," I Meant "I Don't"..153
High Maintenance Farm Girls..156
Running Behind..159
Persimmons & Cat Hair..161
Baby Puke & Salesman...164
Lucy's Laundry Scheme..167

The Farmer

'Beautiful' Holiday Moments	173
Electronic Sentiment	176
Farm Commodities & Indecisive Squirrels	179
When is it Ripe?	182
Weed it and Reap	185
Without Farmers	188
Private Detectives and Toenails	191
Car Fliers	194
Little Jack Horner's Cantaloupes	196
Dead Sheep & Candy Canes	199
Melon Vision Goggles	201
A Combine, A Dresser & a Lawn Mower	203
Financial Advice from a Pug Dog	206
Say Your Pwayers, Wodent	209

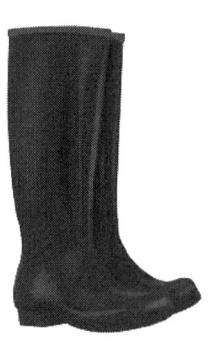

The Farm House

Grandma's Ketchup Soup	215
Life is Like a Box of Crayons	218
My Bon Bon Life	221
Shampoo & Horseshoes	224
The Procrastination Tree	227
The Story of Your Dash	230
The Year of Biscuits	234
Well That Didn't Go as Planned	237
Wreck the Halls	240
I am So Thankful	243
Laundry Fund	246
Alzheimer Clutter	248
Mommy Milk Cow	250
Tooth Fairies	252
Tupperware & Socks	255
DeTrimming the Tree	258
Diaper Duty with Dad	261
How to Care for Your Mums	264
The Crisper: Where Good Intentions Go to Die	267
I Fought the Lawn...and the Weeds Won	270

The Fun

It's important to have a twinkle in your wrinkle.

Abstinence Prevents Minivans

*E*veryone learns basic math in high school...but I think somewhere between Math and Health students should be taught that 1+1=5 and a minivan! One of my college friends is currently looking to trade in his man-card for the dreaded, yet fuel efficient, minivan. He and his wife were making a list of all the pros and cons, and somehow hands-free sliding doors and a built-in vacuum cleaner seemed to outweigh a 5-speed and a lift kit.

I have to admit that there was one time we also drove a minivan. It was a few years ago in Florida. We had just come back from the Caribbean, and there was a mistake at the car rental agency, and the only thing they had available was "a lovely maroon mini"...and unfortunately for us he didn't mean "Cooper." My husband grumbled, but what were we to do? It did easily accommodate our luggage, and it had enough cup holders to appease a thirsty octopus. And enough storage to lose all manner of trinkets.

But driving through the Florida Keys in a minivan—even with the windows down—wasn't quite the experience we'd had before as we breezed through the Sunshine State with the t-tops out of our Trans Am.

It got us where we needed to go, we just felt like we needed a bumper sticker that said "we used to be cool!" The best part about that minivan was taking it back at the end of the vacation...after all, what happens in Florida, stays in Florida...and really how many cup holders does one need? You can only drink one beverage at a time.

Not too long ago, after the arrival of their second baby, one of my husbands friend's, David, surrendered his muscle car for the more sensible family van. One afternoon, we had popped in to visit and he was trying hard to convince us just how cool the decision was. He showed us the wi-fi option, and the folding DVD screens for each kid, night lights under the chairs, and a back door that opens and closes with the push of a button.

And on that self-closing back window was a family of stick figures—thoughtful to let others know you're a family man—since driving a minivan often creates the impression of being wild and single.

"It drives so nice, and there is so much room," David kept repeating. "And the gas mileage is great!"

"Well it definitely looks as if you've got yourself a good dependable vehicle," my husband agreed.

"Ya, I just can't believe all the features they put in these things. It's pretty cool." David continued extolling the virtues of the all-amazing mini. It had both AC and DC plugs, it had park assist, the chairs were extra wide, etc.

While our husbands continued talking minivan features, his wife and I had decided on dinner plans, but we found ourselves short a few ingredients.

"Hey David, can you guys run to the store and grab some lettuce and french bread?" his wife asked.

"Sure, no problem," he said, then he turned to me and asked sheepishly, "Can we take your Jeep?"

Dr. Pendyke's Miracle Salve

Mirror mirror on the wall...what the heck happened? This is not what adulthood looked like in the brochure! I've reached the age where looking in the mirror is like checking the news. I know there will be some new developments I won't like: crows feet, new wrinkles, more white hair.

Actually, that's not quite the truth—while I don't spend long in front of the mirror—I have never given my wrinkles more than a cursory glance—they are just smile memories, character lines. They define my journey—although recently that journey has been bombarded by expensive skin care products.

"What do you use for your daily skin care routine?" queried a persistent salesperson.

"Baby wipes, bull grease and sweat." I grinned.

She looked horrified. "On your face?"

I smiled, "arms, legs, face—wherever." While she was racking her brain to decide what sales tactic is supposed to follow that response, I quickly made my escape.

The next time, however, I wasn't so successful. At a dinner party, I found myself trapped at a corner table with an extremely persuasive multi-level salesperson. No matter where the conversation went, she adeptly steered it back to the skin care product she was selling. Guaranteed to lessen wrinkles, tighten your skin, make it less puffy, clear up age spots—basically work miracles—which it should for the price.

"I don't mind wrinkles," I laughed. "I don't even own an iron—why should my face get more special treatment than my clothes? Although climbing in the dryer with a wet washcloth and coming out wrinkle-free and 3 sizes smaller doesn't sound too bad."

Usually sarcasm is my life-ring out of these situations, but this salesperson didn't even blink. When the other two people at the table pulled out their credit cards, I tried to sneak away. But a well placed hand on my arm and suddenly I felt a guilty obligation to open my wallet and purchase my very own bottle of miracles.

Several weeks later, our family was curled up in front of the TV, eating popcorn and watching the Andy Griffith Show. Opie and his friends were trying to sell a miracle salve that didn't work. Barney decides to help Opie get his money back by pretending to be Dr. Pendyke, DVM, who wants to buy all the salve the company can get back—because it cures 'the mange.'

"Why look at that," my husband poked me in the ribs and in the falsetto voice of Dr. Pendyke began "look here at this miracle salve. For the low price of the cost of an airline ticket, you can buy this cream that will do nearly everything—it even cures the mange!" I rolled my eyes and tried to ignore him. But it was hopeless. As if being suckered in to buying the expensive "miracle salve" wasn't enough, my husband made sure to poke fun every chance he got.

If he saw me going to bed at night without putting it on, he appeared horrified.

"Oh no!" he would exclaim, "I think I see new wrinkles!

Maybe we need to get you more miracle salve to stop them!"

Or if he saw me apply it, he would sigh with exaggerated relief. "I am so glad, you are putting that cream on, I thought I detected a hint of mange yesterday!"

"Oh come on, laugh," he snickered, "that was hilarious!"

I raised an eyebrow. "I'm laughing on the inside—so I don't get more wrinkles," I snorted, as I threw the bottle of "miracle salve" at him.

Recently, we were enjoying the sun on the white, sandy beaches of the Caribbean—perhaps a little too much, as our noses were peeling a bit. One afternoon while downtown, a well-dressed young man stepped out of a beauty shop.

"It looks as if you could use some skin care," he smiled, and I self-consciously touched my peeling nose.

"Come, try a free sample..."

I thought he had meant for my peeling skin, but before I had fully comprehended the situation, the young man was applying serum to one of my eyes.

"Your skin could be so beautiful, it just needs a little extra care," he smiled.

"Don't worry," my sarcasm defended, "my other face is in the *photo-shop*."

He looked at me curiously, but totally missed my sarcasm as he held up a mirror and exclaimed "Wow, wow! Just look at that difference. Why you look at least 15 years younger!" I looked in the the mirror. One eye looked tired and puffy. The other eye looked tired and puffy—and covered in a sticky goop.

My husband smirked at me, but before he could make even one silent "miracle salve" reference, the young man had smeared the serum on one of his eyes too.

"Look at that! You see that? Wonderful, amazing! And 10 years younger without a surgical facelift!"

I looked at my husband's face. Bright raccoon eyes from his sunglasses were very visible, but try as I might I couldn't see any difference where the gloppy serum was.

"All these beautiful results for only $1,099!"

My lips twitched up—a thousand dollar cure for the mange. The young man mistook my smile for approval,

"Would you like a bottle for each of you?" he asked.

I shook my head, "I don't know, honey, Dr. Pendyke has us on a pretty strict skin care regimen of baby wipes, bull grease and sweat."

We backed up, trying to retreat. They young man started after us, and we practically tripped over ourselves to get away.

My husband laughed as I began smearing the sticky goop off my eye, and in Dr. Pendyke's falsetto said, "Amazing, just amazing, not only do you look 15 years younger, but I think you finally got rid of the mange!"

Kids, Parties, & Toothbrushes

*S*pending the summer behind a wheel: tractor, combine, swather, forklift, or pickup, our social interaction is limited, and my 7-year-old spends most of his days reading to my 7-month-old. So when we accepted a birthday party invitation, my son was very excited to get to play with his friends. And I was...well...I was happy that he was excited.

The day of the party arrived hot and sunny. "How many more Scooby Doos?" he kept asking. (His own invention for telling time. 1 Scooby Doo = 30 min.) 12 Scooby Doos, 8 Scooby Doos, 5 Scooby Doos, 2 Scooby Doos, then finally the awaited hour arrived, and we headed off to socialize with parents we didn't know—we could hardly wait.

We smiled and nodded and listened to the latest baby product recalls, the newest baby food trends, and nap time schedules...my husband and I kept looking at each other, we were out of our depth. We drifted around, but none of the topics seemed to include commodity prices, equipment breakdowns, or what the export market was doing. So many of the conversations seemed to include something like: "All my children's snacks are organic, GMO-free..."

"Cool," I would say, then mutter under my breath, "My kids eat 'conventional' candy off the floor...."

Soon it was time for cake and ice cream, and my husband was generously helping himself to our son's plate of dessert. "Do you want your own plate?" someone asked.

"Nah, I'm just teaching him about taxes by eating at least 38% of his ice cream." he teased. More weird looks.

The cake and ice cream were soon devoured, and then we watched as the kids laugh and giggle and dance around and shout stories and anecdotes to their parents. I was longing for the quiet of my tractor cab, and as I looked over at my husband, I saw the same look of child-exhaustion in his eyes.

Now don't get me wrong, I love kids...in small amounts and low decibel levels. I'm sure there were other tales being told, but the loudest ones seemed to fall something along these lines:

1. "Daddy!!"

"Ya Bud?"

"Can you [scour the house, looking everywhere for something I'm poorly describing, that you've probably never seen or heard of before]?"

"I don't know. Go ask your mom..."

 2. A animated child, talking very loudly, in a language only decipherable to his parents. And the parents looking at you like "Hang on guys, I think my kid is getting to the good part of his four-hour long story and we shouldn't miss it..."

I nodded at the parents, I smiled at the kids, and inside I was covering my ears and craving the peace and solitude of a tractor cab.

I finally got some time away from the kids. One whole Scooby Doo—it would have been longer, but my husband found me crouching behind the garbage can, and dragged me back to the screaming, ice cream covered, happy rug-rats running around doing unexplained kid things, and indescribable kid levels. And as I watched my own 7-year-old chasing around, I decided kids are a lot like used toothbrushes: your own is okay...but the idea of someone else's...?

Farm Hair Don't Care

I have always fancied myself a soul from the '50s. With TV role models like Mr. & Mrs. Cleaver, Andy Griffith and Aunt Bee; music from Elvis, Chuck Barry, and Jerry Lee Lewis.

Sometimes I imagine myself living in "the good old days," but then I remember that women needed lipstick and town gloves to be properly dressed—when I step out the door to face the day, I check for sunglasses and a pocketknife—to me that accessorizes any outfit.

Years ago, a Mary Kay salesperson was encouraging me to wear more makeup, saying how much more confidant I would feel. One look at the price tags, and I knew she was right—I would feel confidently broke! Attempting to say no, I told her I preferred the natural look. She quickly flipped through a few pages and showed me 18 cosmetics I could use to perfect the 'all natural' look! My mouth smiled, my head nodded, and my brain silently screamed "if I'm going to paint something, my husband has a whole fleet of implements that could use another coat of John Deere green!"

But, the lack of sophistication in my morning make-up routine may be the cause for my recent string of skin care vexations.

Let me start at the beginning. Earlier this year, a cousin pointed out that I have finally been blessed with white hair. In that moment I experienced the first 4 stages of grief: denial, anger, bargaining, and depression. I tried all summer to get to stage 5—acceptance—without success. Then one morning, standing in front of the mirror trying to assure myself there were no new ones, my husband made all the frustration go away.

"They're not white hairs," he said, "they're wisdom highlights!" So he sports his "chrome" beard, and I have my "wisdom highlights" and all is okay again...until my birthday. I must have triggered a magic number in a data base somewhere, because everywhere I go I am bombarded with skin care, wrinkle cream, and anti-aging serum.

My skin care rituals are pretty minimalistic—usually just a baby wipe before bed—I've never thought of this as laziness—I like to think of it as energy-saving mode. But maybe it's not working as well as it has in the past. After one salesperson worked especially hard to get me to buy their product, I have to say I took a good long look at my wrinkles in the mirror that night. Time may be a great healer, but it's a lousy beautician.

The weeks passed with more sales people trying to sell me skin care. And I kept making flippant comments like "who needs that when I can wake up like this?" Then last week, after a straw delivery I stopped at a local department store to pick up some essentials.

I was wearing dirty blue jeans, cowboy boots and a shirt that probably still had a little straw stuck to it. I rounded a corner of the store with my cart, and that's when it happened—I inadvertently made eye contact with a cosmetic saleswoman. I quickly attempted to correct my mistake, but

I couldn't get the cart to change direction. Before I knew it, she had pressed a box into my hand.

A product valued at the low price of only $199. "It's supposed to clean and hydrate, and exfoliate," and every other wonderful thing skin care products can do. I wanted to throw the box down and run, but instead, I stood rooted to the spot, nodding politely. My brain was still screaming run, when she took a cotton ball and dabbed some of the miracle goo on it. She pushed up my sleeve.

"Let me show you how much this stuff cleans," she announced as she wiped the cotton ball across my arm. The arm that had been hit with a rotten cantaloupe while picking melons, had been covered in sweat from loading hay, and the arm that I'd held up to deflect the dog slobbers from the hound. I held my breath as she held up the dirty ball of cotton.

"See?" she said triumphantly. "Just look at all that dead skin residue that this will remove! Most of us don't realize just how much dirt stays on our skin which contribute to fine lines," she continued on. "That's why this stuff is so amazing..."

Honestly, I was surprised it wasn't dirtier. Those baby wipes must do a good job after all. "Isn't it just terrifying how much debris is on our skin?"

We had just come back from my husband's 20-year high school reunion, and what's really terrifying, to quote Kurt Vonnegut, "is to wake up one morning and discover that your high school class is running the country."

Compared to that, what are a few wisdom highlights and twinkle wrinkles? Those little lines that scurry all around my face...they tell the story of my life—all 38 years of it. I'm not opposed to skin care, but next time I receive before and after photos of the latest in skin care revolution—I just may start humming "maybe she's born with it...maybe it's an instagram filter..."

Hieroglyphic English

"I thought a thought. But the thought I thought wasn't the thought I thought I thought." My son just looked at me like I wasn't thinking clearly. Of all the subjects in school, English was definitely the one we both found the most challenging: I to teach it, and he to learn it. Holding a degree in English and having a bit of experience teaching high school English had me more confident and less prepared for our actual experience.

Rule: When two vowels go a walking, the first one does the talking. As in boat, or train. Except when they don't as in double or howl.

Rule: ie says I as in pie or allies. Except when it makes the E sound like chief or reprieve.

Rule: The i says i in words ending with -ild or -ind: wild, mild, bind, kind. Except wind, unless it's wind.

Rule: if a root word ends in a consonant, double it before adding the suffix such as plan/planned, sip/sipping, fat/fatty. Except in the case of words like fasten/fastening, glisten/glistened, canter/cantered.

Rule: The letter C is pronounced K as in camel or caramel unless it sounds like cyclone

Rule: G is pronounced guh as in gears or gaffe, unless it's giraffe or George.

Rule: the g in gn is silent in gnu, gnaw and sign. Yet if the g and n occur at a syllable break, it becomes signal, and indignant.

When we got to the silent letters, my son looked up from his book "Why do they even bother putting on a letter if we have to ignore it anyway?"

How do I answer that? I have no idea. I've always just accepted it. But why? What purpose do all the silent letters serve? My son sat looking expectantly at me.

"Yes, English is weird. It can be understood though, through tough thorough thought." He wasn't impressed.

And that was just one of many baffling English moments we have had over the last year and a half.

Plural words are also fun. Man is Men, but Pan is not Pen. Foot is Feet but Boot is not Beet. One is That and Three is Those. Box becomes Boxes—but Ox becomes Oxen. I have laughed at these oddities before, but never before was I trying to explain them to an inquiring 7-year-old.

Struggling with the suffix "o-w" I started punching him playfully every time it came up in our reading to help him remember "o-w says (ou)ch."

But then he said that "row should be R-O-E, not R-O-W, because it says O, not OW." True...but....it just doesn't. Not a great answer—not even a good answer. But I barely understand digraphs and how syllable breaks and letter clusters change letter sounds myself—how can I explain it to a second grader. Our book continued with the story of King Tut's tomb—pronounced toom. Here we go again. Womb says room, tomb says toom, bomb says boom....Oh wow. That example blew up in my face.

Then there is the emphasis on certain syllables to make

different words: In a minute I'll examine this minute sample. I'm not content with the content of this book. I object to that object.

There are double words as in the sentence: "all the faith we had had, had had no effect on the outcome of his life."

We have noses that run and feet that smell. Slim chance and fat chance mean the same thing—but wise man and wise guy don't. A house burns up while it burns down. There is no egg in eggplant. Hamburgers don't have ham in them. We recite at a play and play at a recital.

And we haven't even started on the letters that sometimes say different things entirely. I once saw a sign that read: "GHOTI says fish."

G-H as in Cough

O as in Women

T-I as in Nation.

I'm starting to see the appeal of hieroglyphics.

Fitbits & Fatbits

It's spring. That means the tractors are coming out of the sheds, the irrigation pipes are getting set up, and I'm seeing the results of my winter hibernation and delicious holiday baking. The stamina I had in November is gone—along with last year's tan.

We haven't even laid out a single piece of irrigation pipe yet, and already my wrists are screaming in protest, and the backs of my thighs are practicing their cramping skills.

My 90-year-old grandmother-in-law doesn't have this problem. Rain or shine, summer or winter, she walks 10,000 steps every day. She's in a competition with some of the rest of the family, and she'll often be found checking her steps against theirs on her Fitbit—a piece of technology I don't have.

I guess I'm behind the times, even cows are now sporting Fitbits. I do have a few fatbits though, that seem to give me much of the same information. They'll let me know when I've walked too far, run too fast, bent over too many times.

And while they won't give me an exact count on my breathing—they'll sit me down, and let me pant it out if I've overexerted myself.

The sun is shining, and the plow is getting hooked up to the tractor...and the pipe trailer is getting hooked up to the pickup. I've been dreading this moment. Laying out pipe is my least favorite job. I looked longingly at the tractor. "Oh no!" I gasped, with melodrama, looking down at my feet. "I 'forgot' my rubber boots! Guess that means the tractor-driving job is mine?"

There is really nothing like spring-time ground work. Seeing the dark lines of fresh, damp, soil turn over in long rows is exciting. A little country music on the radio, some toys for the kids on the floor of the tractor—it sure was good to be back in the sun.

We weren't the only people enjoying the warm day. A group of bikers went by, and not far behind them a couple of runners, then a lady jogging behind a stroller, and a couple of teenagers walking a dog.

Boy, I could use some exercise too, I thought to myself, looking down at my 'winter thighs.' It's not because it runs in my family—those winter thighs happen because no one runs in my family!

My sister painted a picture to hang over the tub in my bathroom. In the same font as the "got milk?" commercial, it reads "get naked." I may not have a Fitbit. I may not walk 10,000 steps a day. I may enjoy that Christmas fudge a little more than I should. I may have a bit more thighs in spring than fall. But at the end of the day, when I get naked in the bathroom—the shower still gets 'turned on.'

Curious Parker & The Man in the Yellow Hat

My mom has said she should have named me George—not after my paternal great-grandfather but rather after the curious rascal monkey. However, that wouldn't make any sense, because he lived with the Man in the Yellow Hat—and I live with my parents and my big brother. I am 15 months old and my name is Parker.

I do feel like George sometimes though. He is always trying to do good things, and it's not his fault when they don't turn out right. My Momma is always asking us to help clean up the house. So after getting chocolate all over the TV remote, I thought I would help by washing it.

I dropped it in the water, but it didn't come clean—so I thought I'd just let it 'soak for a bit' like Momma does with the dishes. Then my brother came in and saw what I was doing. Instead of smiling he started hollering.

I don't know what he was so worked up about. I was standing right there watching the remote, it wasn't going anywhere. Suddenly, my parents were there too, and before I knew it, I was whisked out of the bathroom.

I heard Momma groan as she pulled the remote out of the toilet. I didn't have any better luck when I tried to wash her hot rollers. Now the bathroom is off limits to me. I just don't understand, I was only trying to help her clean like she had asked.

I try to help in other ways too. Our dog is getting older and I keep hearing my parents say we have to watch her food—make sure it's good enough for her. I tried to help by sampling it. It smelled pretty bad, and I couldn't help but make nasty faces.

I crammed my cheeks full of soft beef chunks in gravy. It made me want to gag, but for the good of the dog I tried to keep it all in. Even when my Momma came running in shouting, I squeezed my eyes shut and willed my tongue to swallow.

Before I could decide if the food was "good enough" or not, my Momma had her finger between my teeth and was scraping it out. I tried explaining how I was helping the dog—but for as old as they are, they aren't very fluent in baby.

Momma washed out my mouth and face, and when I was clean again, she plopped me on the floor with a bowl of apple slices. I think the dog should skip her food and come eat mine—it tastes a lot better.

To save time, I tried to get myself dressed one morning. I went to my dresser and started looking at my clothes.

What to wear? The white shirt? I pulled it out of the drawer and tried to press it on my head. I pressed and smashed. No luck. It must be too small. I tossed it aside.

I tried the blue one. Same thing. And the green one. I decided all the shirts in that drawer were too small. I know that Momma likes to take out the clothes that don't fit anymore to make room for the bigger ones.

I thought I would save her some time, and I unloaded the entire contents of the drawer onto the floor. When she saw me, she had the same look as the Man with the Yellow Hat when he sighs "Oh, George..."

I tried to help load the dishwasher too. I filled it full of all kinds of dirty things: shoes, coins, pencils, and my sippy cup. I managed to get the detergent out of the cupboard and climbed onto the door and sat down next to the soap dispenser.

But that's as far as I could get—that stupid cap was so stuck I couldn't open it. That's when my Momma came in. I tried to ask her for help, but she was already scooping me right off of the door. She plopped me on the floor and I watched sadly as she undid all of my hard work and reloaded it with just dishes.

My efforts don't seem to go unnoticed so much as unappreciated. I tried to help Daddy take bolts off the rototiller, I tried to reorganize his tool box, I tried to prime the grease gun...and each time I got pulled away and set down far away with some really dumb toys called "Plastic" and "Unbreakable."

It wasn't my fault I dropped the screwdriver down the air vent—the cat scared me. I didn't mean to lose the kitchen door knob either. It just came off in my hands. I took it because I thought it might open the bathroom door. When that didn't work I just put it somewhere—if I could remember where, I would get it—really I would.

I see that look on her face again. It really does look just like the Man in the Yellow Hat. Kind of a mix between sad and frustrated and maybe a little upset. But I wasn't doing anything bad. I was just dumping this basket into the garbage can. You always say you hate this "Bill Basket." I was trying to make you happy.

You know, maybe I should get you a yellow hat for Mother's Day.... Then you could look like the Mom in the Yellow Hat. I think the blanket in the spare room is just the right shade of yellow too.

Conned with the Truth

I once read that *fear is a darkroom where negatives develop.* One only has to pick up a magazine or newspaper to find that fear in so many articles. Fear sells. Fear of wrinkles sells beauty products, fear of being stranded sells roadside assistance, fear of burglary sells home security systems.

Agriculture is no stranger to this fear either. Fear of pesticides push people to buy organic, and fear of the unknown causes people to reach for the "non-GMO" label.

Some fear is good. It warns of danger and can help keep us safe. But there are very few monsters who warrant the fear we have of them. Take for example dihydrogen monoxide (DHMO) or hydroxyl acid. Perhaps you've heard of it: it's colorless, odorless, tasteless, and kills uncounted thousands of people every year.

It has a pH level of 7, and is a main component of acid rain. It is deliberately sprayed on organic crops. It is dumped into rivers by big companies and never degrades. It corrodes metal. It is used as a cleaning agent in mortuaries. Water bottles stored on shelves longer than a month have been found to have high levels of it. It is used in industrial solvents, nuclear power production, as well as an ingredient in most baby foods.

Each year, dihydrogen monoxide is major contributor to millions of dollars in damage to property and the environment—most recently effecting Texas. Contamination has reached epidemic proportions. Quantities of dihydrogen monoxide have been found in almost every stream, lake, and reservoir in America. The pollution is global, and the contaminant has even been found in Antarctic ice.

Prolonged exposure to its solid form causes severe tissue damage. Symptoms of ingestion can include excessive sweating and urination, and possibly a bloated feeling, nausea, vomiting and body electrolyte imbalance. It has addictive qualities, and for those who have become dependent, DHMO withdrawal means certain death. 100% of all people exposed to DHMO will eventually die. Afraid yet?

The government has refused to ban the production, or distribution of this chemical due to its "importance to the economic health of this nation." Several individuals have tried petitioning for bans.

One of which was 14-year-old student, Nathan Zohner, of Idaho. He actually had more than 85% of his classmates sign the ban for eliminating DHMO. For which he won first place in his science fair and actually had a term coined after him. "Zohnerism," wrote journalist James Glassman, "[is to] refer to the use of a true fact to lead a scientifically and mathematically ignorant public to a false conclusion."

For what is dihydrogen monoxide (DHMO)? It is two hydrogen molecules, and one oxygen—in other words. H_2O. Water. All of the previous facts were about water. Are they facts? Absolutely. And there are more. Starbucks serves thermally agitated dihydrogen monoxide in many of their beverages and it may cause burns if it contacts skin. *Hot water can burn.* Prolonged exposure to solid DHMO causes severe tissue damage. *Frost bite.* Gaseous DHMO can cause severe burns. *Steam is hot.* All of this is factual. But it's silly once one realizes DHMO is just water. And if all of that could be said about water, what else are we letting fear scare us from?

One of my favorite acronyms for FEAR is—*False Evidence Appearing Real.* Before becoming afraid of food—whether you choose to eat organic or go GMO—take a moment to see behind the 'facts.' Who's feeding the fear? What is their agenda? Make your decision to continue to use DHMO or not, based on your knowledge and common sense—not just what your neighbor does or what you see on TV.

A man walks into a bar and orders H_2O. A second man says "I'll have H_2O too." The second man dies. Just parroting your neighbor can have dire consequences as the second man here discovered.

(H_2O_2 is the chemical equation for hydrogen peroxide)

Surfing the 50-50-90 Rule

*E*ver heard of the 50-50-90 rule: Anytime you have a 50-50 chance of getting something right, there's a 90% probability you'll get it wrong. And get it wrong I did... over and over. We have been encouraging our oldest son to try skiing this summer. He is extremely cautious when it comes to water, and hadn't shown much interest in trying a new activity—tubing or using his trainer skis seemed to be enough.

I can see myself in him as he hesitates to try anything new—especially when it isn't possible to try it out in private first. Nothing worse than test driving a new piece of machinery with half a dozen eyes on you—just waiting for a really stupid mistake.

So when he asked to try kneeboarding alone (not behind the boat), I understood.

One day early this summer, I was given the opportunity to wake surf. A sport I have never tried and have only watched a handful of times. Now you already know that I don't enjoy learning something new in front of people, but

I also hate getting in the water.

Don't misunderstand—I love water and water activities—but getting in is the worst part about them. Unless you are scuba diving in the tropics, the water is chilly and cold—and did I mention it isn't very warm? Even in 100 degree weather I am wearing a wetsuit—I'll take the teasing over the cold any day!

I looked at the surfboard. Half of me wanted to try, the other half said I was crazy for even thinking about trying something new in front of a boat full of spectators. I was waffling.

Then I saw my son. I decided that if I expected him to learn new things, I could at least attempt to be an example. And an example I made too—of what not to do!

I suited up, and pushed off the back of the boat with an unfamiliar board and a ski rope. I listened carefully to the instructions, moving the board where it belonged and holding the rope just right.

"Okay!" I nodded to the boat driver.

I learned to ski when I was 10 years old, and consider myself moderately water-athletic—I got this.

Well, what I got was a nose full of water while the board shot up over my head and landed 10 feet away. The boat pulled around again. I pushed my wet hair out of my face as I repositioned the board.

Dan, the friend who had encouraged me to surf, kept giving me advice and support: "When you feel pressure on the board, just push your knees up, then hop up onto your feet."

I nodded. I felt pressure on the board...I got my knees on it...then my right foot...then my left—a mouth full of water. Again, pressure, knees, right foot, left—crash. Over and over and over. I crashed forward, backward, sideways...I drank water, snorted water, coughed water...everything but getting up on the water.

I'm not sure how long I was out there—but I know it was long enough I didn't have to worry about hydrating the rest of the day! After a particularly painful crash, I laid my feet up on the board while the rest of me floated in the water.

"Hey, why don't you try it like that?" Dan teased.

Sure, why not? I thought, it can't hurt any worse—and that's when I got up. Within minutes I knew this was going to be one of my new favorite water activities.

Give a girl a surfboard, and you've distracted her for a day, Teach a girl to surf—and suddenly work becomes the distraction! I have never tried to get my swathing done as quick as this year—get it done—catch that wave!

As the summer progressed, Dan and his wife began encouraging my son to try surfing. He generally just ignored their attempts at getting him on that board. One day, however, he seemed less reluctant than usual. He still didn't want to surf, but he asked to play with the board in the water.

Soon someone threw him the rope and we started pulling him slowly through the water. He used it as a kneeboard for a bit, that he laid back down and motioned for the boat to stop. He said he wanted to try standing up. Two attempts and he was standing on top of the water. I was one seriously proud Momma!

Later that day, my husband, who has never skied or wakeboarded, announced that he wanted to try as well.

"If at first you don't succeed, we have a lot in common." I smirked at him.

Happy to see him try, yet getting the camera out to capture some epic crashes. He got the same instructions I had earlier this summer. They tossed him the rope...he hollered "hit it"...the boat took off...my finger poised on the camera—and he got up. The first try!

My first reaction was shouting hurray...followed by a

close second of "I was in the water how long?"

"Sometimes it's not about how good you are, but how bad you want it." he smirked.

I set down my camera and picked up my soda. I guess he'd never heard of the 50-50-90 rule. I wonder if he heard about the guy who got hit in the head with a can of soda? He was lucky it was a soft drink.

Passport Photo Resemblance

Clean socks and perfectly coiffed hair are no match for a missed connection, a rerouted red-eye flight, a rental car, and a taxi. 29 hours after leaving Portland, we finally landed in Louisiana, via Washington D.C. By the time we stepped out of our last transportation connection, haggled and groggy, we looked just like our passport photos.

Orson Wells once said there are only two emotions in a plane: boredom and terror. Especially on a red-eye; everyone is turned and twisting trying to find a bit of comfort in the possibly 3 inches the seat reclines—which might be delightful if one were a horse that enjoyed sleeping upright. You close your eyes praying that your exhaustion will allow you sleep away the flight.

Just about the moment your body starts to relax, the plane plunges forwards and jerks you against the seat belt. That's when your brain splits. One side tells you all is fine—after all they are still serving beverages. The other taunts, yes but listen, the captain is on the intercom "flight attendants please take your seats."

The turbulence continued to get worse. To my left the wing jerked unpredictably, to my right, an African woman clutched a chain of beads, chanting in what could only be described as a terrified plea. With no comforting place to look, I closed my eyes and did what I suspect many passengers were doing. Promising God a little something if we made it safely onto the ground.

But I guess it wasn't too bad...if you define it by the negatives. We didn't get hijacked, we didn't crash, we didn't have to use the barf bags, we didn't lose our luggage, we didn't miss our cruise. So with the exception of the resemblance to our passport photos, all was good.

As we were going through the embarkation line, we began chatting with the couple beside us: comparing places we'd both been. They had a bucket list of places they would still like to go. They asked us how we picked our destination. We have a little travel book. It makes nearly all our vacation decisions, choosing between Amsterdam and the John Day dam. We call it our checkbook. This year is Central America.

We were all excited: I was excited to see new countries, my husband was excited to return to favorite locales, and my son was excited about the food on the ship.

Our cruise started out like any other vacation...unpacking more clothes than we would wear, shoes we didn't need, and books we hoped to read. Getting our stateroom in order really worked up an appetite, so we headed to the buffet. After which we played a life-size game of chess on the deck—which really made our stomachs growl. I'm not sure how many times we sat down at supper that night (I may have intentionally forgot), but we definitely did not go to bed hungry.

The rest of the vacation was amazing as good holidays should be. We rafted underground rivers, we ziplined into caves, rode dune buggies in the mud, swam with sharks, kayaked over tropical reefs, and visited Mayan ruins, all the while making ourselves frequent visitors to the dining hall.

As like the rest of my life, I lugged around a camera (or 3) for every moment on the cruise. I see life through a viewfinder. Without a shutter button to click, I feel the way some women describe being without lipstick.

My brother contributed to my disease by giving me a new GoPro for Christmas. Like many other new electronics, it didn't come with a user's manual, instead it listed a website where I could download my own. The GoPro had three buttons. How hard can it be? I thought, as I added it to my other cameras and gear.

I first used it while snorkeling with the sharks. I pushed and clicked away and was very pleased about some of the close-ups I was getting. Imagine my horror when we went to watch the footage, and realized that I had "on" and "off" backwards.

Each time I had a good shot of a shark I turned it off. What I did have were lots of fins and bubbles and legs of people I don't know. I learned a painful lesson that day. Owning a GoPro doesn't make you a videographer. It makes you a GoPro owner.

As we drove home from Portland, loaded down with stories, souvenirs, (and less video than I'd expected) my husband reached over and took my hand.

"I love traveling with you," he smiled, "I hope we can travel the world together. You know why?"

"Why," I ask, squeezing his hand and smiling.

"Because if anything ever happens to me, you won't be able to travel to new places with someone else."

My husband may no longer look like his passport photo.

You Know You are from a Small Town When...

I recently picked up an article entitled "you know you're from the farm when..." I settled down in my chair and prepared for a few minutes of amusing light reading.

It started out with "...you have only 2 McDonald's in town." Only *two?*

I read the next one "You casually state to out-of-towners that your house is protected by the Good Lord and a gun, and you'll meet 'em both if you show up without welcome." Okay, I'll give them that one.

But when I came to the third I had to wonder if the writer had ever even been in a small town.

"You know you're from a small town when your school tardiness is excused because your combine only goes 35 mph."

Huh? 35 mph? In a *combine*? And a tiny town with *two* McDonald's? The article should have been titled "you know you're not from a small town when you think...."

The rest of the statements were equally ridiculous. "Yeh frequentleh tahlk with that old suthern drawl laihke this, an' nobody gits tired of it. And them city gals just melt when yeh use it."

After shaking my head, I decided to just write my own hopefully with a bit more accuracy.

You know you're from a small farming community when...

10. Your short cut across town is avoiding the stop light

9. When you look up at the sky, you see familiar constellations, and aren't surprised that it's dark enough to see them.

8. On a grocery trip, you buy all your frozen foods last... to ensure they won't melt on the way home.

7. You're in the city center and you can see or smell cows without walking too far in any direction...and you think nothing of it

6. You have (or know someone that has) had a lamb or calf in the bathtub ...and you're wondering now why that would be unusual.

5. It's time for roof repairs and you bring out your front end loader to do the job.

4. Your early morning prayers always mention something about rain.

3. Your chain saw gets used for everything from house remodels to cutting down your family's Christmas tree.

2. You wear specific hats for farm auctions, cattle sales, and holidays (and they probably all advertise a local business).

And the #1 way you'd know you were from a small farming community...if you saw a combine coming down the road at 35 mph, you'd get out of their way in a hurry...because you'd know they must have lost their brakes coming down the hill.

Boys and Their Dogs

*S*pike came to live with us when he was 11 weeks old. A bumbling puppy hidden behind a mess of wrinkles, sagging ears, and huge paws. He looked like a child playing dress up in their parents closet—his skin draped over his face and puddling under his chin. When he looked up at you with those big, sad, drooping red eyes, you couldn't help but want to pet him...and laugh. It was our first experience with a blood hound.

We brought him home and watched as he tried hopelessly to climb the steps, his enormous paws throwing him off balance. He backed up and tried it again, this time whimpering loudly when he stepped on his own ear causing him to come to an abrupt stop.

He was a bumbling 20 pounds of puppy and my son fell in love before the evening was over. It took a little longer for my husband and me to feel the same, for a 20-pound puppy comes with little sharp teeth and a large, weak bladder. I had seen full-grown dogs leave smaller puddles. 1 hour + 3 ruined socks + 5 puddles = a frazzled mother with no puppy love and a new home in the barn.

My 10-year-old Great Pyrenees turned up her pretentious nose at the slobbery, smelly, mischievous ball of pup my son named Spike. As did the cats—they stormed around for weeks expressing their displeasure at the goobery gas bomb.

But my son loved him. Day after day they rolled and tumbled, and dug holes and chased sticks. The ring around the bath tub in the evening often reflected the amount of fun they had had.

As the months passed, both boy and pup grew...although the pup outgrew the boy in no time at all. Soon the pup weighed in at over 100 pounds...in part, no doubt, from all of the items he would steal and eat: hats, sunglasses, sandals, ball bearings, ropes, garden hoses, motorcycle helmets, and bike tires.

Every time he does something especially naughty and my patience seems about frazzled I watch boy and dog dig for gophers. Both down on all fours, with dirt just a flying (mostly from Spike's shovel-sized paws), often making bigger holes than the gophers ever would, but they come up with such satisfied expressions, I can't help but smile.

It's a wonderful example of how a friendship should always be. Each truly believes the other belongs to himself. Spike gives his boy rides like a mini pony, and his boy in turn rubs him down and gives him treats. The boy used his egg money to buy his dog a bed, and Spike in turn lets the boy sleep on it with him in his dog house.

Wanting a dog that does tricks, my son spent hours (and several boxes of Cheez-its) and finally can make his dog sit and occasionally lay down. But like everything else in their relationship, it is a two-way street.

Spike has now taught my son how to bay like a hound, he says he can speak dog really well now, but he doesn't always understand it.

And last night he curled up on the dog bed with one of my

favorite blankets and fell fast asleep. I almost didn't have the heart to disturb him...after all, he had circled the bed three times before finding the exact spot to sleep in.

My Uncle's Uterus

They say the definition of insanity is doing the same thing over and over and expecting different results...I'm betting they started dusting off our straight jackets with the appearance of that second pink line.

It was the beginning of my fifth pregnancy. Only one child to show for all those months of vomiting and headaches...and we were trying again? Insanity at its best.

The next month we stumbled through our routines, with but one thought on our minds: "Will it keep?"

Too soon, complications arrived, and I suddenly found myself staring up at my ceiling day in and day out, thinking that a straight jacket probably offered more freedom.

Harvest started and soon I began hearing farm machinery outside my bedroom walls. My husband texted me pictures of how the plants were looking, and how the hay was cutting. Even bringing me in fresh cut silage to smell.

I couldn't decided if it was worse to see what I was missing out on or not. I've heard people joke about being so bored they watched the grass grow, but for the next 6 weeks

I really did watch the corn grow through my bedroom window. I "measured it" against the spots of texture on the bedroom wall.

Those long weeks weren't entirely valueless though, I learned:

1. It is possible, in the event of extreme down time, to get tired of reading.

I would have never before imagined this possibility, but never before had I knocked out 600 pages on a daily basis for weeks on end.

2. Some people's recommendations for books is astonishing.

I read some great books, I read some terrible books, and I attempted some books that I'm not sure I'd ever be bored enough to finish. I asked the friend who brought one such book how she had enjoyed it.

"I don't know," she answered. "See that bookmark?" She pointed to the one about a third of the way through the book. "It took me about 2 years to get to there."

Oh, that makes sense now, I *always* recommend books I didn't enjoy enough to finish. Yes, I'm still scratching my head.

3. Love isn't the big things…it's a million little things… even shop items.

I am a shower girl. Baths are fine, but after all day in the heat and the dirt, the idea of swimming around in all that mud isn't my idea of a clean time. But I found myself too dizzy to stand for a shower.

My husband, farmer that he is, quickly remedied that situation. He brought in a 5-gallon bucket of hydraulic oil and put a towel on it. Instant shower chair. Love in the little things.

4. Crocheting is an art—and I am no artist.

My aunt thought this would be a great time to learn to crochet. She supplied me with *How To* books, yarn, hooks, and lots of beautiful patterns.

The first pattern in the "Easy to Learn Crochet" book was a small potholder. I carefully wrapped the yarn around my fingers just like the picture showed, and there I sat, my fingers all tied up in yarn.

For the next hour I wrapped that yarn around everything but my head—and that was contemplated. Four hours later I had a misshapen 'square' with dropped stitches, added stitches and had my husband in stitches when he saw it.

Needless to say, no one will be receiving beautiful scarves for Christmas....not to say they won't get scarves, they just won't be *beautiful* scarves.

5. Great friends are like four-leaf clovers, hard to find, but oh so lucky to have.

Within days of being confined to bed, I received a care package from a far away friend that contained books, tea, bath salts, and a few issues of Vogue (because maybe in my downtime this farm girl could absorb some fashion—I am sure I will disappoint my friend).

Some of the girls from the youth class I taught at church brought me over chocolate-dipped strawberries and played with my son all evening. Other friends brought over house cleaning fairies, cooked food and one offered up his massage skills.

One especially amazing blessing came from a friend who drove all the way to Nevada to bring home a baler we had purchased—and detailed my pickup in the process.

Another friend loaded up our sprayer and moved it for us.

At the end of an exceptionally stressful week of hemorrhaging, my uncle even offered up his uterus. I was so touched. If he ever gets prostrate cancer, I'll be first in line to offer up a replacement. Of course he threatened to forever call my child Utie if it's a girl or Ute if it's a boy. Maybe I'll have to rethink this exchange!

I'm not sure what will happen with this pregnancy. I'd like to think "it'll keep." But no one can write their autobiography in advance.

We may be insane, and intentionally captaining our ship into stormy waters, but it has been a blessing to discover friends who didn't hesitate to be a lighthouse to us.

And come November, the Lord willing, we'll be able to sail back into safe harbor with a little babe and forever get rid of those crazy straight jackets!

Calendars, Storks & Redneck Labor

    *E*veryone familiar with the Gregorian calendar, knows that all months contain between 28 and 31 days. Even school children who maybe haven't been taught yet about the Roman calendar and the Julian calendar and the purpose of the leap year, probably still know the little rhyme that sing songs:

Thirty days hath September,
April, June, and November.
All the rest have 31,
Except for February all alone,
It has 28 each year,
but 29 each leap year.

Being a rational person, I have always believed this rhyme. But it is wrong. So very wrong. I am willing to bet that I am not alone in that belief. I think all months have between 28-31 days in them...except for the last month of pregnancy. At which point, time seems to replicate faster than Borg nanites, making that final month closer to 473 days. And you can't help but think the stork has gotten lost.

As your due date approaches and disappears, (just like the tips of your shoes), family, friends, the clerk at the convenience store, start gazing at the big watermelon you're swinging around, and ask "What are you going to do?"

Like it's just a big blister that I can soak in Epsom salts and make it go away. Trust me, for each time someone has thought that baby should be arriving soon, this expectant mother has thought (and dreamt) it 10 times.

And each time it gets said, the idea of castor oil niggles ever more slightly in the back of my mind. Of course, castor oil and prune juice I think should be left to people with much stronger stomach muscles and intestines than I have.

But castor oil aside, I live on a farm. There has got to be all sorts of Redneck Remedies for getting this baby here sooner.

My husband jumped right on this train of thought. For each day I remain pregnant is one more day he has to be the primary caretaker for my pregnant ewes. Forget forceps, he says with glee, there are calf-pullers. And one doesn't need the vacuum extractor at the OB's office, he's got a Shop-Vac with loads more horse power.

If baby is stuck, there is PB Blaster that is sure to do the trick. Combine that with a few shots of WD-40 and baby shouldn't even make a squeak after it comes out.

Need to walk that baby out? No problems, we still have plenty of winter watering to finish up. No need to walk without an irrigation pipe in your hand. A little gentle exercise to help work those muscles? The hay trucks are coming daily, and he can always use an extra grunt on the trailer to move those bales into place.

And don't worry about running out of breath, while you're loading the trucks, he can bring along the portable air compressor and just hook me up.

It was about that moment that he started gesturing to the welder. Before he could say a word, his phone rang, interrupting the next helpful solution.

It was then, I had an overwhelming desire to buy a bottle of castor oil. I think it might actually make a really nice addition to my husband's dinner plate tonight...then we can both hold our stomachs tonight and commiserate on how long and uncomfortable that last month of pregnancy really is.

All Ya Gotta do is Act Naturally...

"You have been invited," the cardboard cereal box said "to come find out who shot Cletus in the butt." It was a hillbilly themed dinner party mystery and we had been asked to go as Bubba and Emma Jean.

Now I love a good dress-up party, but on a Sunday in the middle of harvest? My husband and I were still on the fence as to whether we could spare the time, when the host texted to tell us she'd even bought Legos for our son. Who can turn down Legos?

So we RSVP'd and quickly forgot all about it. The Sunday dawned bright and sunny...and incredibly busy. It wasn't until half-way through the afternoon that we remembered we had a party to attend that night.

I got home before my husband and I stood looking at our closet. Similar to when I'm hungry and I stand in front of the fridge waiting for a homecooked meal to jump out of the drawers and cook itself.

I had about as much luck with the clothes in my closet. They had the audacity to just hang there and ignore me.

I looked down at the tattered jeans I was wearing. There was a big spot on the bottom where I'd stepped in an over-ripe cantaloupe that morning while picking, and there were sticky streaks across the right side where I'd wiped watermelon juice off my pocket knife, and they had more patches than my grandmother's prized quilt.

While I was waiting for inspiration to hit, I thought I'd at least comb my hair. The hound had started baying at o'dark thirty this morning, and I'd pulled it into a pony on my way out, and never thought about it again.

Oh boy, one look in the mirror revealed dirt and grease marks on my face, and hair that could use a good shampoo. I glanced at the clock about the time I heard my husband come in the house. We had 10 minutes. There was no way we'd have time for much of anything. My husband peaked his head into the bathroom...he was even dirtier than me. He'd been replacing a bearing on the header of the swather and looked like the grease gun had fired off a few rounds.

"I gotta take a shower," he said pulling stalks of hay out of his hair and off of his shirt

"We don't have time," I said, wrapping a handkerchief over my dirty hair. "We're just gonna hafta go or we'll be late!"

My husband grabbed a wig, some fake black teeth my dad had bought him that he's been dying to use, and a straw hat that he haphazardly fastened on.

On our way out, I saw a Sharpie laying on the counter and I figured we had time for a couple of quick "tattoos." We grabbed some guns on the way out of the house and as we were headed down the walk, I saw a rope the dog had drug in.

"Here, quick, let's make you some suspenders," I suggested. Which we tied on and ducktaped in the back. And we were off. Bubba and Emma Jean.

My husband was a little disgruntled that we hadn't

dressed up much....or even cleaned up for that matter...but at least we were on time.

We walked into a party that had been decorated with old couches, clotheslines, old whiskey bottles, a wading pool, possums, and all manner of other redneck, roadkill stuff. People we were accustomed to seeing in suits and ties were dressed in denim and straw hats. As I sat down in a thrift store recliner in the yard, and my husband sat on a toilet seat lid, we began the game in character. After the first Act was over, the hosts played a set of mini games. One of which included best hillbilly award.

Imagine my husband's surprise when he won the best dressed award! As we drove away that evening with our "prizes," (mine a roll of toilet paper, and my husband's a gold plastic "emmy") we didn't know whether we should be proud or ashamed, that with no time and little effort, we'd brought home prizes....

But we weren't going to let that toilet paper go to waste. It is after all the middle of harvest, and the roll in the stack truck is getting a little thin....

Marriage Talk

"Dearly beloved, we are gathered together here, in the presence......." No. Too stuffy.

"Friends, Romans, countrymen, lend me your ears...." No. Too ridiculous.

"Welcome." The white screen mocked me. I was putting together my first wedding ceremony. I'd recently been asked by a cousin to officiate at her wedding and I wanted it to be perfect—for a few reasons: 1. How many times would I have the privilege of marrying a couple in my lifetime and 2. She may never speak to me again if I blow her special day.

I sat at my screen for another hour before sighing and hitting the delete button. My piano teacher always used to say "Open strong, end strong. If you're going to mess up, do it in the middle, where people are less likely to remember." I needed the opening to be perfect. But nothing seemed to work. My husband came in about then and asked me how it was coming.

I lowered my voice and quoted Princess Bride "Mawwiage. Mawwiage is what bwings us together today. Mawwiage, that bwessed awwangement, that dweam within a dweam..... In other words," I said, "not well. I'm just about ready to begin 'Marriage, the final frontier. These are the voyages of the bride and groom. A continuing mission to explore strange new worlds, to seek out new life and new civilizations...to boldly go...." My husband's look stopped my trekkiness dead in it's shuttlecraft.

"Well, if you won't help with the opening," I said, "perhaps you could help with the 'keys to a happy marriage' part. What advice would you give a couple embarking on a new marriage?"

My husband leaned back against the counter, and looked into his glass of water. After a thoughtful pause he said, "If you must argue. Argue naked."

Now it was my turn to give him a dirty look. "I'm serious!" I grumbled, throwing a kitchen towel at him.

"You wanna 'fight'?" he asked wickedly.

"Shoo shoo shoo!" I hollered, opening the kitchen door, "back to work for you!! I have a ceremony to write!"

Today, there will be no dearly beloved, no betrothed, and no ancient rime of the mariner. Today, there are no dead languages to solemnize vows that are very much alive and will remain so for a lifetime. Today, promises become permanent and friends become family. Today is about love.

Finally the words were coming, I continued typing, but I couldn't get my husband's "advice" out of my head. As crazy as it was it held a little water. Arguing naked would limit your arguments and there would certainly be less heated discussions about GMOs among the community.

I soon started on my 'keys to a happy marriage.'

1. Love your differences. Opposites really do attract. If you marry someone exactly like yourself, one of you is unnecessary.

2. Forgive. Live in the present. What went wrong in the past is the past. You create the present and future with your thoughts, words, and actions right now. Choose them wisely.

3. Love leads to commitment.....and it is commitment that will eventually lead back to love.

I didn't include arguing naked to my list of 10. But it certainly gave me some thought for the rest of the afternoon. Along with other inappropriate for weddings, yet sometimes sage advice on marriage.

The grass is always greenest where you water.

Your neighbor's yard may look greener...but upon closer inspection...it's astroturf!

Don't have breakfast together. Few people are at their best in the morning.

Correct his driving. How will your husband know he's going too fast unless you continuously slam the imaginary brakes on the passenger side of the car?

A wise physician once said, 'The best medicine for humans is love.' Someone asked, 'What if it doesn't work?' He smiled and answered, 'Increase the dose."' I now pronounce you husband and wife, you may kiss the bride.

I smiled as I hit save, my ceremony was all written, now to go find that husband of mine and clear the air!

Spring Diet Duet

It's spring. And that means farming is in full swing, gearing up for a busy year. Irrigation is running, the equipment is being pulled out of the shop, the animals are heading out to summer pasture, and everywhere you turn you see itty bitty, teeny weeny, little polka dot bikinis. That's right, it's swimsuit season.

Not wanting to miss out on the pain of swimsuit shopping, I found a black and white polka dot one I liked, and went to try it on. I quickly realized my caloric intake outnumbered the polka dots. Guess it's time for a little spring cleaning... starting with the refrigerator.

My husband came home just as I was starting the cleansing process. "The horror," his face seemed to cry. And that began our spring diet dialogue.

Me: We're overweight.
Him: We're under tall.
Me: Nothing wrong with exercise.
Him: Nothing wrong with extra size.
Me: We should work out more.
Him: We should cook out more.

Me: The road to health is paved with good intentions.

Him: The road to the kitchen is full of new dimensions.

Me: Here's a dumbbell.

Him: You are the dumbbell.

Me: How about a stationary bike?

Him: I just sat in a stationary car...

Me: Buns of steel.

Him: mmmm...buns...of cinnamon...sugar...frosting

"Well at least you'll never have to worry about your abs of steel setting off the airport metal detector," I snorted at him.

"I don't need exercise," he told me, "I already have the body of a god. It's not my fault you don't like Buddha."

I rolled my eyes.

"I don't need to limit my dairy," he continued, "because I'm saving up for a triple bypass. So why should I exercise? When I can just save up for a lap band?"

The only exercise my husband seems to enjoy is side stepping the issue, pushing his luck and over-working his brain to think up excuses for not having to work out.

That evening I went jogging alone, all the while thinking about that cute polka dot bikini. After all, running is a strenuous exercise which would help convert fats, sugars and starches, into aches, pains and cramps. The next day I was going to go jogging again, but as I picked up my sneakers, my toes voted against me 10 to 1. I may have flabby thighs, but at least my stomach covers them.

The next morning, I finally found an exercise we could do together: up, 1,2,3, down, 1,2,3....then the other eyelid.

Sardines and Baked Beans

*O*nce upon a time, several years before I was born, two people tied the knot and were enjoying a honeymoon road trip. During an otherwise forgettable gas station stop, something happened that created a story that will likely be passed down for generations.

Being hungry, my dad asked my mom if he should grab some sardines and crackers for them to munch on.

"Whatever you want," she told him. Arriving back at the car with sardines and crackers, he was surprised to discover my mom hated sardines, and was just planning on eating the crackers.

The story goes that a heated discussion ensued: my dad not understanding why my mom hadn't just told him what she would like to eat, and my mom not understanding why it was a problem for her to just eat the crackers.

That little miscommunication at a fuel station nearly 40 years ago has done several things: 1. It became part of our family legacy, 2. It made sardines and crackers the logical gift to give my parents for their anniversaries, and 3. It made us a little more aware of how we communicate with our own spouses. Or so I thought until last week.

My husband and I were heading north to attend our niece's 6th birthday party. The day's farming had been one near disaster after another, making us leave many hours later than expected.

Half an hour into our trip, our stomachs began growling and we realized in our haste to get stuff done and get on the road, we had skipped both lunch and supper. We had a scheduled stop to pick up some kayaks for the kids, and as we stopped, my husband asked what he should grab for food.

"Anything," I replied, "I'm starving."

"Baked beans?" he asked, thinking about the case he knew was inside. It is a food he loves and I abhor.

"You know, I'm just about hungry enough," I laughed, before he closed the pickup door.

A few minutes later he returned and handed me a Gatorade, and some fruit snacks and set an opened can of baked beans on the dash. He loaded up the kayaks while I munched on the fruit snacks. He got back in the pickup and pulled a plastic spoon out of his shirt pocket and into the beans.

As we backed out of the driveway, he handed the can to me—presumably to hold until we got back onto smooth roads. The sweet pungent smell wafted up, souring the taste of my fruit snacks.

I held them until we hit the highway.

I held them until we got through the next town.

I held them until we had passed the town after that.

Finally, I asked him "when are you going to eat these?"

"Oh I didn't bring them for me, I got them for you?" he explained sincerely.

"But I HATE baked beans. You know that." I exclaimed incredulously.

"Yes, but you said you were hungry enough to eat them,

and there wasn't much in the cupboards."

"It was hyperbole! I'm so hungry I could eat a horse. I'm so hungry I could eat baked beans?"

My husband stared at me blankly. "Well if you wanted something different, you should have said so."

And suddenly I looked at my can of beans and saw a 40-year-old dispute. They say the apple doesn't fall too far from the tree...I wonder if you could likewise say the sardine doesn't stray too far from the baked beans?

Forgotten Father's Day

The calender seems to fly by so quick, and the days are crammed with farming from predawn to—well, sometimes predawn the following day.

So it is often easy to overlook such inconsequential things such as breakfast, kids in the bathroom, mowing the lawn and shaving. You can nearly judge just how busy and/or stressful the farming season is by the length of the "chrome" growing on my husband's face (he refuses to call it gray).

The busier the farming season gets, the more things fall into that inconsequential category. But some things will never fall there, no matter how busy one is: coffee, sunglasses, coffee, feeding the kids, coffee, and major holidays (if parts stores would close for birthdays and anniversaries they would have a better chance at being remembered too).

So when my husband got a phone call from his Grandmother, it wasn't too surprising when she began reprimanding him for forgetting something—it is farming season after all.

"Neither you, nor any of your brothers called to wish your dad happy Father's Day!" she scolded. "Such ungrateful children," her voice implied.

My husband listened quietly, and then replied calmly "Well, when Father's Day rolls around next Sunday, I'll make sure to wish him a happy day."

"It's always graduation weekend and you missed it. Not one of you four boys even called him!"

"I'm pretty sure it's this coming Sunday," my husband replied, "because no one wished me happy Father's Day either."

The line was quiet a minute, and you could almost imagine her flipping through her calendar before she realized he was correct. Father's Day hasn't yet arrived.

Every once in a while, you get in trouble for something you didn't do, but it's rare that just a lowly calendar can pull you out of the fire.

After the initial laughter had subsided, my husband had to call his dad, letting him know he wasn't forgotten.

"I'm just not used to wishing you "happy Father's Day" more than once a year," I heard him say.

So, in case the rest of the week gets so busy that we "forget" again, here's a special shout-out to both my dad and my father-in-law. Happy Father's Day!

How could we forget the people that bring the most humor into our lives. We're thankful for all the laughs you provide us—hopefully one day you'll find the memories funny too!

Joe's Buffalo

I squinted hard, and could barely make out the 5 on the clock's little hand. I rubbed my blurry eyes. What was that noise, that very loud noise, a deafening, earth shaking noi—then I woke up enough to recognize the phone. THE PHONE?

Suddenly I was wide awake. What was wrong? Who was calling? Was there an accident? Did an animal get out? Get hit?

My sleeping brain went into overdrive with horrible, tragic, wild thoughts.

Then my husband mouthed the words: "Everything's fine. It's just my brother. Go back to bed."

I laid back down, my heart still racing, and adrenaline surging...I was awake. And not because of a new baby, or the cats fighting, or a problem with the sheep...no...I was awake because my brother-in-law forgot about the time difference between Colorado and Oregon.

"A buffalo?" my husband exclaimed, eliminating the last chance I had at sleeping. I couldn't help but listen to his side of the conversation.

"Why would you buy a buffalo?"

"Because your dog died?"

"You thought you'd replace your lab with a buffalo?"

"But you live in Denver! What would you do with it?"

"Put it in your backyard?"

"A city ordinance, huh?"

"Only a goat, no other farm animals?"

"Huh, imagine that...not being able to have buffalo in your tiny backyard..in Denver?"

"It's just a baby? You KNOW what babies do, don't you?"

"Oh, but it was at an auction,"

"Oh yes, of course, I get it. You HAD to bid on it...the buffalo being at an auction and all."

"$900 seems a great price for a baby buffalo, to replace your lab that died, that you can't put in your tiny backyard because of a city ordinance, in the small rural town of DENVER!"

By now, I'm holding my sides from laughter. I'm not much of a morning person, but this was worth waking up for.

"You want me to take it?"

"What would I do with a buffalo?"

"...I stand corrected, 'baby' buffalo?"

"Just feed it and bury it when it dies?"

"Oh, well that's making much more sense. Bid on a buffalo to replace your pet, to send to your brother who lives 16 hours away, so we can feed it, and care for it, and bury it when it dies.

And since the buffalo is 16 hours away from you, so it can't greet you when you come home, and you can't take it for walks (in your small rural community), you'll just get another dog to replace the absent buffalo, that you bought to replace your old lab."

"Only you, Joe!"

Thankfully he lost the bid later that day, and no buffalo arrived, baby or otherwise...but I started thinking about maybe auctioning off my barren goat. After all, goats meet Denver city ordinances.

She Thinks My Tractor's Sexy

*A*pril Fools. A much loved holiday in my house. As a child my dad would wake us up from bed by hollering about the spiders running across our pillows. As we got bigger, so did the jokes.

In high school, a friend and I found ourselves in charge of the hot lunch meal on April Fool's Day. It took us a while, but we made cupcakes for the school kids—beautifully frosted cupcakes made out of kitchen sponges.

A few years ago, my husband and grandpa collaborated on a prank that my parents didn't discover until the following day. On April 2 my parents received a phone call from the neighbors. The neighbors had talked it over all night, and they figured they could buy my parents place and rent it back to them until the farming improved.

My dad, having taken the call, was confused to say the least...until the neighbor told him about the For Sale sign my husband and grandpa had hung near the road.

On the way home from church another April Fool's day, my husband started checking out a tractor parked in the corner of a field with For Sale written on the windows. He was getting excited about the cheap price on the window, until he recognized the tractor and read his own phone number on the glass.

We have a hard time letting a funny moment pass us by. That might be why my mom and I found ourselves dying whitey-tighties for Easter this year, while most people were dying eggs. Surprisingly though, the men in the family weren't nearly as excited about wearing their BVD's as we were about making them. Laughter is the glue that holds our family together.

This year my husband has decided to put his "Fooling" effort into my dad again. My dad's favorite joke at the moment goes something like this:

A farmer was having his morning coffee when he leaned up against the sink and looked out the kitchen window.

He'd recently purchased a new John Deere tractor, and he'd parked it in the backyard. He was pretty pleased with his purchase, and was enjoying the morning sunlight reflecting on the green paint—when suddenly he saw a naked man dancing around it.

The farmer snorted coffee as he watched the naked man gyrate around the front end weights. It was a train wreck that the farmer couldn't tear his eyes away from.

When the naked man started brushing up against the tires, the farmer couldn't take it anymore, he headed out to see what was up.

That's when he met Bill.

Bill and his wife had been having problems, and that's when Bill agreed to see a counselor.

Bill told the farmer, "and the counselor told me to do something sexy to a tractor."

The farmer looked confused for a moment, before he smirked at the naked man and repeated "to attract her."

With that joke in his mind, my husband has been cutting,

decorating, and painting materials to "primp out" one of my dad's tractors. Even going so far as to make big lips and doe-like eyes.

He left home at 4 in the morning, to be at my parent's house early enough to decorate up the tractor before my dad would wake up. He put up eyes and lashes in the windows, earrings on the mirrors, bright red lips on the front end weights, a black lacy skirt, and even a pretty flower on her exhaust stack.

So if anyone sees a "sexy" tractor in Eastern Oregon, don't spit your coffee...just send them better marital advice.

The House that Peter-bilt

This is the house that Peter-bilt.
This is the transmission that quit in the house that
Peter-bilt.
This is the tractor that housed the transmission
That quit in the house that Peter-bilt.
This is the trailer that attached to the tractor
That housed the transmission
That quit in the house that Peter-bilt.
This is the telehandler with the broken horn
That pushed the trailer
That attached to the tractor
That housed the transmission
That quit in the house that Peter-bilt.
This is the sheep with the lamb just born
That crossed the telehandler with the broken horn
That pushed the trailer that attached to the tractor
That housed the transmission
That quit in the house that Peter-bilt.
This is the maiden all forlorn

That yelled at the sheep with the lamb just born
That crossed the telehandler with the broken horn
That pushed the trailer that attached to the tractor
That housed the transmission
That quit in the house that Peter-bilt.
This is the farmer that grumbled and moaned
That kissed the maiden all forlorn
That yelled at the sheep with the lamb just born
That crossed the telehandler with the broken horn
That pushed the trailer that attached to the tractor
That housed the transmission
That quit in the house that Peter-bilt.
This is the For Sale sign, all new in the morn
That lessened the farmers grumbles and moans
That kissed the maiden, no longer forlorn
That smiled at the sheep with the lamb just born
That crossed the telehandler with the newly-fixed horn
That pushed the trailer that attached to the tractor
That housed the transmission
That quit in the house that Peter-bilt.

The Frustration

God gave us shin bones
so that we could find
trailer hitches in the dark!

Word Processors & Funerals

*W*e've all heard it—the best way to really understand something is to try teaching it. I believe I can take that thought one step further—you never really understand something until you can explain it over the phone to your grandmother.

My Grandma was a prolific writer, and was constantly writing new poems or stories either by hand or with her typewriter...then my aunt set her up with a computer and word processor. Her new 'toy' gave her renewed joy at writing, and nearly doubled our phone conversations.

"Hi Bri, this stupid computer...how do you change the space on the indent?"

"Hi Bri, this stupid computer...all of my text is italicized, what do I do?"

"Hi Bri, this stupid computer...I thought I'd saved my poem, but I can't seem to find it...HELP!"

She tested my knowledge of word processors often, and sometimes for long periods of time. But she would liven up potentially boring conversations with random bits of trivia she'd just heard

(one acre of soybeans can produce more than 80,000 crayons);

off color jokes

(a granddaughter living with her grandmother kept wearing revealing clothes. After several futile talks, the granddaughter came downstairs to see her grandmother topless. Horrified, she asks why,

"Well honey, if you want to let your rosebuds out, I thought I'd put out the hanging baskets.")

And of course her latest poems:
> *"You can say round or pleasantly plump*
> *too much size to the thighs,*
> *too much lump on the rump*
> *doesn't matter how you cut it,*
> *does no good to sugar coat it*
> *fat's fat, and that's that."*

You never knew what you were going to get, or how many hours it would take when Grandma called to ask for computer help—but you always got off the phone with a smile.

She has been gone nearly 2 years now; last week would have been her 80th birthday, and what I wouldn't give for another long phone conversation starting with "Hi Bri, this stupid computer..."

My grandfather also passed away this spring, and as families do, we cried, and laughed, we cried some more and we tried to make light of the fact that we will all someday be pushing up daisies.

It was during some of these lighter moments, that I realized our family has a really morbid sense of humor.

My uncle wants his ashes to be flown over his son-in-law's strawberry farm—"I want him to know he took my daughter, and for that I'm going to be everywhere he is—literally."

Next time I eat strawberries labeled 'organic,' I'm pretty sure I'll taste nothing but ash...

My cousin wants to skip the funeral and have a wake—I don't think he's listened to Ray Steven's 'Sitting up with the Dead,' or maybe he has, and he wants to leave his wife a new set of french doors for the kitchen.

The song starts with his 97-year-old uncle dying. He was so stooped over they used logging chains to straighten him out. It is 3 a.m. And the family is all sitting around when the thunder causes the chain to snap and old Uncle Fred just sat right up.

Well when Uncle Fred sat up so did everybody there and there came a great partin' of the foldin' chairs.
The preacher nearly knocked me down, he said
"I'm headed out that kitchen door over there."
I said "Rev, that kitchen ain't got no door in it."
He said "Don't worry son, it will have in a minute."
And I ain't sitting up with the dead no more,
'cause the dead started sitting up too!

My husband wants a crank to put at the end of his closed casket. And as everyone files out past him, they have to take a turn at it...and he wants it to sound like the children's jack-in-the-box toy as it turns. I'll never think about pop-goes-the-weasel the same way again!

If only my Grandma could have been privy to these conversations she would probably have outdone us all on the morbid craziness, and I'm going to guess it would have had nothing to do with a 'stupid computer'—unless it came with a big hammer and cell phone...

Carrots, Eggs & Dead Crab

*A*ll things are possible with coffee and cowboy boots...at least that's what I told myself as I threw a bag full of toys and snacks into the swather for the kids. Swathing has got to be one of my favorite jobs—I think the only task I enjoy more is driving forklift.

Things were going smoothly—the kids were happily entertained, there was an enjoyable program on the radio, and there were minimal gopher mounds in the field I was cutting—in that moment life was perfect.

Then a funny thing happened. *Bang!* The platform to the right of the cab appeared to break. I stopped, but other than having fallen a few inches, it looked okay. Odd, but nothing too serious.

A few more rounds and I noticed it had fallen even farther and was now starting to rub on the inside of the tire. I stopped—time to call in help.

Ten minutes later my husband looked miserable as we stared at a broken drive hub. The platform hadn't moved at all—it was the whole wheel that had tilted sideways—

a long and expensive fix. I packed up the toys, coffee thermos and kids and we all piled into the pickup.

My husband looked dejected. This spring had been so wet it had been nearly impossible to get into the fields—and now that we were in, we were broke down. Sometimes farming is like playing 5-card poker with 4 cards.

As we drove home, my husband started listing all the things that were broke or in dire need of attention. It reminded me of a story my Grandmother used to tell.

"Everyone in every walk of life faces hardships and adversity—it's how we react to them that changes the outcome," I told my husband. "If you were to drop an egg and a carrot in boiling water, the egg would toughen up, and the carrot becomes mushy and gross."

My husband rolled his eyes "what about the crab that just turns red and dies?"

"Ahhh. You're ruining the analogy. There's no crab. Carrot or Egg. You can only pick between the two," I give an exaggerated sigh.

"Okay, I pick the egg," he smirks at me, "because then you can have deviled eggs for lunch!"

Analogies can be cute—but sometimes boiling water just brings out the wicked in us!

A few hours, several phone calls, and a lighter pocketbook later we were bringing back a new swather to finish out the first cutting. I threw in the bag of toys and a new thermos of coffee and climbed into the freshly Armouralled cab.

The kids immediately started pressing handprints into the shiny glass windshield while I enjoyed the easy straight lines that auto-steer provides.

I began thinking about eggs, carrots and dead crabs—and I realized that my grandmother left out an integral part of the story—coffee grounds.

You don't have be a mushy carrot, a deviled-egg, or a

dead crab. When faced with adversity you can smile and use that hot water to make coffee. Add cowboy boots, and a pocket knife—and all things become possible!

Fifty Shades of Hay

"Uh-ooooooooh," my toddler sing-songed as he picked up his little green, toy man with suction cup hands and feet and stuck him back up on the swather window. The toy would soon start sliding down, then lose all suction and fall.

"Uh-ooooooooh," my toddler laughed and scooped up the toy again.

This game went on for hours—which was good because we were hot and heavy into second cutting. My toddler does a lot of jabbering, but the only words he says are Keeg (for his brother),and Bama, (which means food—any kind of food: dog food, cat food, sheep food, baby food, etc.). So this new addition of "Uh Oh" seemed pretty cute—that is until it became apropos.

Sometimes farming feels like playing pinochle with old maid cards...and this week was no exception. It seemed that instead of moving from hour to hour, the week was passing from one calamity to the next.

The swather lost a bearing, bent a roller, plugged up, and

found a broken mainline—buried it up to it's axles in unexpected mud. "Uh-ooooooooh."

The baler broke all 6 knotters at once, and then twisted the safety linkage. "Uh-ooooooh."

The stack truck blew a front tire, and the four-wheeler a back one. "Uh-oooooh."

The hydraulics on the straw swather refused to work, the rake lost a wheel, and I cracked the screen on my phone. "Uh-ooooooh."

It felt like we were playing a round of the Farming Game, where you draw operating expenses for each crop but without receiving your harvest check. Someone needs to throw that card away and slip in an extra couple "double all your corn harvests this year" squares or at least an extra O.T.B. or two.

You can't tell how good a man or a watermelon is until they get thumped...and I'm starting to feel punky with a hint of "uh-ooooooh."

The higher the mercury gets, the more temperamental my swather becomes. After plugging up badly—the hay wrapped tightly around the full-contact rollers. I climbed back into the cab like a damsel in distress, waiting for someone to come bail me out of my predicament. My toddler sat on my lap and pointed at the lifted flaps on my header. "Uh-ooooooh," he crooned.

"Yep, 'Uh-Ohhhh' is right," I replied, wiping some of the dirt off of his cheeks. "Kind of reminds me of a nursery rhyme," I told his upturned little face.

I changed some of the words to fit this particular scenario, as I recited: *"There was a little swather, who had a little crack, right in the middle of it's windshield. And when it was good, it was very very good, and when it was bad—it was HORRID!"*

Okay, so Henry Wadsworth Longfellow it is not, but that's how I felt. When it was working it worked beautifully...and the rest of the time was just a series of "Uh Ohhhhs"

Ever wonder what happens when you cut the opening rounds of a field and have a breakdown, and then a few inside passes and a breakdown, and a few more passes and another breakdown? You get '50 Shades of Hay.' It's a lot more "stemmy" than its "steamy" counterpart, and isn't nearly as profitable!

The little green man fell from the window again, breaking my thoughts, "Uh-oooooooh" my little guy laughed as he scooped up the toy. I sure hope he learns a new word soon. I don't know how much more we can afford this one. Perhaps with just a little tweaking on his pronunciation his "Uh-ooooh" can say "Ua Pou." Maybe that's actually what he's been getting at all along—with every breakdown, he just wanted us to think about a beautiful tropical island in French Polynesia.

If we're going to spend a ton of money, while sweating profusely, at least we can do it in swim suits on a white sandy beach...not in work boots, ordering parts for a persnickety swather while rivulets of sweaty mud drizzle into your eyes and your nails get torn by pulling out clumps of alfalfa between obstinate rollers.

Next time I hear "Uh-oooooh," I'm going to envision the beautiful rocky spires of "Ua-Pooooou."

Save a Horse, Drive a Tractor

Snow blew onto my helmet and I had to keep wiping my shield to see where I was going. Not that it mattered—my job was only to steer and stop—the little yellow rope connecting my snowmobile to my husband's snowmobile was really what determined the speed and direction. This was the second time in a week that my sled had made the "tow of shame" back to the trailer.

The day was a beautiful one. We packed a picnic lunch, the kids, and the snowmobiles up to the mountains for an afternoon of family fun. As we pulled the sleds out of the trailer, I looked questioningly at my husband as he chose the new, red one over the trusty, blue one.

"You sure we wanna take that one up again?" I asked—last weekend fresh in my memory. We had recently upgraded my sled, and on its second ride out, we'd stopped to take a few photos—and it never started again. Thankfully, another group of snowmobilers stopped and offered to help haul the kids and the persnickety sled back to the trailer.

During the week, we had the carburetor cleaned, and it

was running like a champ—in the trailer. I was however, dubious.

My husband assured me that it was running great, and he wasn't worried in the least. Sometimes I think that women worry as much as they do, because men don't worry at all! But regardless, between the two of us, he is the mechanic, not me, so the red one it was.

I took one last overdramatic glance at my old trusty blue sled, to which my husband gave an eye roll—exaggerated enough to be seen even through his helmet.

"It'll be fine!" he shouted over the running engines. Oh to have those words dubbed over the sound track of the next few hours!

The snow stopped blowing against my helmet as my snowmobile came to an abrupt halt. My husband had stopped. He stepped off his sled, "Mine's starting to overheat," he explained.

His sled is water cooled, and the trail didn't have enough powder on it to keep his engine cool. Add the extra weight and pull of another snowmobile and it exacerbated an already hot situation.

We untied the tow-rope, and he took off with his hot sled into the deep powder to cool it down. Ten minutes later he was back, we reattached mine and soon the snow was pelting my helmet visor.

Tow, overheat, unhook, cool down, hook up, and repeat. The kids didn't seem to mind. They took each overheating opportunity to build forts, or tunnels, or snow chairs.

Truthfully, it wasn't too bad until the sun went down. Then, each time we stopped to let his sled cool down, we all cooled down.

While we were waiting, the kids and I would jump and wiggle around to keep our fingers and toes warm. All that jumping must have shook lose some old memories. For I suddenly recalled an old family story that had been passed down through the generations.

My great-grandfather had traveled west, making his home in Idaho raising mules to work the grain fields. After a terrible fire destroyed his business, he took his youngest children and moved to Eastern Oregon where he began growing watermelons in 1934. Thus began the Walker family legacy of farming watermelons. While we still hold to that heritage, our methods are quite different.

My great-grandfather used horses and mules to farm, and my grandfather didn't see any reason to change something that had worked well for centuries.

One day, he was plowing a 40-acre field that had grown a lovely crop of sand burrs. He was using a young horse that seemed especially high-strung. The horse wanted to get out and go, and pulling a slow plow through the field wasn't his idea of a good afternoon. My grandfather discovered that if he unhooked the horse at the end of every row and let him run for a few minutes, he would pull the plow a littler easier.

At the end of one of the rows, the horse was especially antsy. My grandfather unhooked the horse from the plow, but while he was still harnessed to the horse, the horse took off. As the story goes, my grandfather got a real close up of that 40 acres of sand burrs.

By the time the horse had cooled down, my grandfather had heated up. That was the last day the Walker family farmed with horses. That horse went to sale, and my grandfather bought one of those "new-fangled" tractors.

My husband rode up on his sled, his "horses" being cooled off, and began attaching the rope to my plow of a snowmobile. I looked around the dark outlines of trees and piles of snow, there were no sand burrs in sight, but I suddenly had an overwhelming desire to go tractor shopping.

The Toilet Paper Stay-cation

It was a week of the unbelievable. It started with my husband installing a fresh roll of toilet paper on the dispenser, (he usually just sets it on top of it) and ended with him hanging sheetrock for the new toilet paper holder.

For Christmas my husband surprised me with tickets to the Caribbean. Ever since my parents let me head off to Israel and Africa when I was 14, I can't seem to travel enough and thankfully, my husband enjoys traveling as much as I do. My hands shook with anticipation as I looked at the departure date: January 4.

There was much to be done before we could leave: hay to be delivered, bags to be packed, and of course that is the week we would end up with a bummer lamb. So a housesitter needed to be found to feed the dogs, cats, and lamb.

The day of our flight dawned gray and dreary, but our spirits were high—soon we would be resting our tired bodies in the warm salt water of the Caribbean.

Only an hour into our trip to the airport, I started to feel queasy. Soon we were parked at a truck stop, while I sat on the concrete in front of the pick-up with my head between my knees. I was green. It was a stop and go trek all the way down the gorge.

"I can't get on an airplane like this," I moaned. My husband agreed readily. He makes no bones that he "*doesn't do gross,*" and puke definitely falls in that category for him.

While parked along an off-ramp with my head hanging out the door, he called the airlines to see about postponing our ticket 24 hours—and that's when the unbelievable week hit a new gear.

We had already missed our flight. It had left at midnight the night before. We were stunned. In all our crazy adventures around the world, we had never misread a ticket so completely!

Before I could get too upset about it though, my stomach muscles constricted and I stepped out of the pickup again. Maybe this will be better, I thought, we can get a hotel, get rid of this bug, and reschedule in the morning.

The next morning, I felt weak and dehydrated, but at least I didn't feel like I had to get better to die. My husband was sitting at the desk, phone to ear, shaking his head, just like last night. He covered the mouthpiece.

"There are no flights out due to the storms on the east coast." That couldn't be right. I grabbed a tablet and within minutes found a flight leaving from Boise. "Try to book it," he said discouragingly.

I tried and received an error message. Over and over I would find tickets but they all disappeared in error messages. We sat in that hotel room searching for flights, talking to airlines, airports, and travel agents—all with the same result.

There were no flights in the next 5 days to Puerto Rico. A knock at the door from management reminded us that we had overstayed the extended checkout. It was a somber trip to the parking lot, towing luggage packed for a tropical getaway.

We continued the phone calls all the way home hoping that perhaps we had overlooked something. No such luck. The fog and snow swirled around as we drove the last few miles to our house. I normally love winter, but when you have envisioned your evening on the hot sand with coconut oil and bikinis, the ice and fog just seemed to taunt us.

I started unpacking, and to keep from moping began to declutter and before I knew it, I had a stack of boxes ready for Goodwill. The cleaning bug was contagious, and soon my husband and I were both tackling our nemesis—the basement. The place full of our "have-to-haves" that seems to multiply exponentially. We found boxes of his old computer games on the original 5-inch floppy discs.

"But those are classics," he said as I added them to the trash. My 8-year-old dug them out to look.

"Wow that must be a really big computer to take those, they wouldn't even fit in my Kindle."

As our "stay-cation" continued we revisited our years-old remodel projects. We sheet-rocked, taped, painted, hung lights, and tiled. In my married life I have never had a laundry room. The washer and dryer just hang out in the play room like members of the family. Now, after all these years they have their own room...it really is unbelievable.

My in-laws once missed a trip to India, and my late mother-in-law took that opportunity to re-paint and re-carpet her house...she would be proud of this effort. I'm starting to think that missing the trip wasn't such a terrible thing after all. My husband doesn't usually put effort into things without a profitable return—like house projects—but this week he made a serious effort.

Almost makes me want to pretend to book a trip, just so we could pretend miss it! But the next time I see the toilet paper roll on the dispenser, (and I didn't put it there), I'm going to get my tool belt out and bring in my air compressor...maybe I'll get that pergola I've been dreaming of.

Do You Wanna Build a Snowman?

"*Do you wanna build a snowman?*" seems to be sung daily at my house. At first it was exciting seeing the snowmobiles parked in the yard. My 7-year-old would rush to the window each morning to see how much more snow had accumulated.

As the weeks passed and the snow piled up, the number of snowmen in the yard seemed to lessen though. My husband and I love snow—maybe even more than the kids—but rolling out of bed, and suiting up for the negative temperatures every two hours to check for baby lambs takes some of the fun out of it. The frigid temperatures seemed to make the snow fun disappear—along with the ears and tails of many of my baby lambs.

One night, my husband brought in a baby lamb that had nearly frozen to death. The whole house went into a frenzy: a hot bath was drawn, towels were heated up, colostrum thawed out, and the baby lamb lay stiffly oblivious.

A sleepless night was had by all, but by dawn she let out a hungry beller. The dog jumped, I cried, and my son delightedly exclaimed, "Now we can name her!" And *Snowflake* was born.

Both my boys enjoyed the novelty of a house-bummer. My oldest taking great delight in feeding time—while my youngest delighted in letting her nibble on his fingers. He reciprocated by nibbling on her ears—and she seemed less than delighted.

More snow kept falling, the temperatures kept dropping, and it wasn't long before Snowflake was joined in morning feedings by Snowball...at least by now, they were both in the barn.

With each passing day, the snow began to have less and less appeal. My boys were still singing "Do you wanna build a snowman..." but I was starting to hum "Winter's a good time to stay in and cuddle, but put me in summer and I'll be a …..*happy momma*!!"

A body can only take so many days of sub-zero temperatures, so one afternoon we packed up and headed south looking for sun and heat. Pulling out of the driveway we slid across the icy road—we were not going to miss this weather. We pulled back onto the road and started the trip again.

The ice made the going slow—but our trip came to an abrupt stop when we got stuck in traffic from a head-on truck accident outside of Shaniko.

We spent the night waiting for the crew to reopen the road. We didn't arrive in Madras until 6 in the morning. We should have just stopped for coffee, but we were just dying to lay down flat and close our eyes. Not knowing where to find a hotel that rents by the hour, we sadly paid full price for just a handful of hours.

The parking lot was a sheet of ice, and for traction they had used cracked corn. At first glance I thought it was an ingenious idea....but weeks later I'm still picking up stray pieces of corn out of the carpet in the pickup.

But we were heading south...away from snow...so what

was a sleepless night, an expensive hotel, and a little corn?

We were nearly to Mexico when we discovered a misunderstanding with our reservations. We found ourselves in Southern California with a day to kill.

We thought maybe a day at SeaWorld would be memorable—after all we had each loved watching the killer whales when we were kids. But SeaWorld no longer has theatrical orca shows due to publicity by animal rights activists.

Perhaps a day at Knott's Berry Farm instead—but no, they were closed due to inclement weather. And what inclement weather it was. It rained. And rained. For days on end.

We splashed our way through Disneyland; we built mud castles on the beach; and we used the hotel dryer nearly every night. We had escaped the snow...but not the precipitation.

The week ended and we had to head home. Out of the rain and back to the snow. We had an appointment to pick up some produce in a little town on our way through. As we got close, the traffic began to get unusually heavy. We soon discovered there was a potential dam break in Oroville and they were evacuating....Suddenly, the traffic made sense—we were right in the path of the mandatory evacuation. Water covered roads, signs, and railroad tracks. Houses, barns and cows stood miserably in glassy water.

The next day we were finally able to leave the flooding area—without our fruit and with a very violent stomach malady. We puked our way down the gorge, in the middle of a terribly foggy night. It was deja vu as the freeway was shut down again due to another truck accident.

We arrived home at 6 in the morning, smelling like vomit and wet cracked corn. We trudged through the snow and into the house making muddy footprints across the black and white tiles. I wish someone would either apologize to Mother Nature...or shoot her pet groundhog! *I don't wanna build a snowman....*

The Sands of Time

*T*ime is my love language. Gifts are nice, words of affirmation are always an ego boost, but it is time that really means the most to me. Time is more valuable than money—you can always make more money, but time spent is gone forever. So when my husband asked me if I wanted to go with him to deliver hay to Grass Valley I didn't even hesitate.

Spending time with my family is one of my favorite things to do: it doesn't matter if we're swimming with sting rays and sharks in Belize, or bottle feeding bummer lambs at home—I am happiest when we're all together.

It wasn't long before the trailer was loaded, the kids were bundled up, and we had a whole stack of books for the trip—we were set.

The trip down was uneventful and pretty—we all enjoyed seeing snow all the way from our house to Grass Valley. We sang geography songs about countries of the world, read another book from the Chronicles of Narnia series, and watched a few episodes of the original Get Smart.

Arriving at our destination, the purchasing farmer pulled

out a sled and pointed my 7-year-old toward his kids' sledding hill. The trailer was soon unloaded, and we started making preparations to head home.

That's when our family outing became an adventure. Just before pulling back onto the road, we noticed the farmer was running toward us waving his arms.

"Your back tires aren't turning," he panted. Figuring them to be filled with snow or ice, we backed up. They released and we started off again. Making it almost 10 feet before the farmer started hollering again.

Forward, backward, stop, repeat. Finally the tires seemed to be loosened and we started homeward. Barely on the road 10 minutes, sparks started to fly, and the smell of rubber permeated the cold air. The axle had locked up again, and what was left of the tires looked like shredded wheat.

The snowy ice crystals along the road somehow seemed colder and less pretty than they had just minutes before—but I didn't need to worry about looking at them too much—the right headlight picked that time to die.

My husband called the farmer, and asked if he had tools to "fix" the wheels. He did, and 30 minutes after we left, we were back in his yard again. I sure am thankful for farmers and ranchers. They so often give their time to help people—even strangers—without a word about their supper that is surely getting cold.

The wheel bearing had burned up, taking with it the spindle and the axle. What was left of the tires was soon removed, and the axle chained up, and our "Clampett-mobile" was soon clippity-clopping back down the road.

By now, it was dark and cold, and I had 2 little boys who were protesting loudly about how hungry they were—I certainly was no Granny, or I could have whipped up some possum-innerds and squirrel dumplings with the 2 hot sauce packets and 1 packet of powdered creamer that I found in the jockey-box.

We usually try to live by the motto *"twice as much time, half as much money,"* possibly because our wallets are like onions—every time we look in them we cry! This trip however, cost us not only time but, twice as much money!

Yet even with all the elements of "adventure" on our trip, I would rather have been there with my family, than on any exotic location in the world alone. They say a beautiful sunset without someone to share it with isn't as pretty. And I have to agree.

I guess I'm a girl with expensive tastes—I'd take time over the most decadent chocolates or lavish jewelry in the world. After all, it's the most valuable thing there is. It's always in short supply and you can never get it back....may we all invest it wisely.

Jim's Drops of Kindness

We cannot tell the precise moment a friendship was formed. It's like filling a vase drop by drop, until at last one drop makes the vase overflow. A series of kindnesses will also at last make the heart run over and you suddenly are aware of your friendship.

Such is the case with a neighboring cattleman. I'm not sure when we first met, nor do I remember when he stopped being just "one of my husband's" friends, but somehow he made his way into my life, my cellphone and quite often into my kitchen—the effects of several of his visits still fill my pantry.

"Hey, Kid," he asked one day, "Ya like onions?" Hardly did I know that my "yes" was going to result in a half a bin of onions on my porch the next day. I dried, froze and ate onions on everything for weeks. Considering that my husband hates onions, I think he was less than appreciative that Jim's generosity gave me onion breath. To which Jim laughed "He's the only vegetarian I know that won't eat vegetables."

Jim often brought us homemade pickles, tomatoes, cucumbers and squash, but his generosity extended far past garden produce—he was generous with his time. That doesn't happen often in this day and age...maybe it never did.

There are never enough hours in the day, especially in agriculture, work is forever calling—but Jim always took the time to answer a call from friends and neighbors. And call they did. Sick, dead, or dying animals—he would be there. Often bringing his wife and whatever supplies he thought you may need.

Bloated cows, dead fetuses, out of fuel, it didn't matter the job, Jim would come if you needed help. Morning, afternoon, or night—friends knew that Jim was just a phone call away. Even on holidays Jim would answer the call.

Thanksgiving day we found ourselves with new baby lambs and no trailer to bring the sheep home. Not a problem, Jim and his wife left their turkey dinner to help us herd sheep in the dark—all the while, smiling and teasing. He'd never begrudge you his help, or make you feel obligated to him. He may cuss at you, but never without a smirk and often a wink

"Hey Kid, what's the Old Man got ya doing now?" Jim asked, his blue eyes twinkling, as he came around the tractor.

"Oh, this stupid knotter just won't tie," I answered climbing down the baler. "I've been fighting it all afternoon."

"You should tell that husband of yours to get his butt in gear and fix it," he laughed. My husband was *'on his way,'* but we both knew that's a fluid time-frame that has it's own units of measurement.

Forty minutes passed quickly though when Jim was around. He'd been around the world and it was always fun to compare places we'd been and the different experiences we'd had.

We always had a good time bs'ing with each other. We'd tell off-color jokes, talk religion, politics, guns, agriculture, wolves...he had an opinion or story about them all, and before we'd know it, minutes would often turn to hours...but at least we had solved the world's problems in the meantime.

He had the vocabulary of a sailor, the wardrobe of a redneck, and a heart to rival any saint. As I stood watching the pallbearers lay down their boutonnieres on his casket, I felt a deep aching in my heart. They just don't make people like him very often. Looking around the tissue-clad attendees, I think the community must have agreed.

The tears continued to fall, and probably will at unexpected moments, but missing someone gets easier every day. Because even though it's one day further from the last time you saw each other, it's one day closer to the next time you will. And until that day, may we take a lesson from Jim and spread drops of kindness throughout our community.

His Version
My Version

*M*y husband and I agree on most things, but occasionally we remember different versions of the same chapter. And I suppose if I were brutally honest, the truth lies somewhere in the middle—although closer to my version, I'm sure.

Night one

My Version: I took an Excedrin pm and went to bed early with a biting headache. I laid motionless for hours, hoping to keep the pain at a minimum. I eventually drifted off into a light sleep.

Which was why my husband's snoring was especially not welcome that night. It kept getting louder and more obnoxious. I tugged at his covers, I kicked his legs, I pushed on his shoulder, all the while repeating his name in various tones.

Suddenly I smelled something funny. I sat up quickly. Too quickly. My headache pounded in protest and I laid back down. I couldn't put my finger on the smell. It smelled hot, but not quite like anything I'd smelled before. Just about that time, my husband stirred.

"Do you smell that?" I asked. He grunted no. "Will you at least check it out?" I asked. Imagine my surprise when he comes rushing back into the room. Our son's giant teddy bear had gotten pushed into the fireplace, and the fur was melting. *I've never been so thankful for snoring!*

His Version: My wife went to bed early, and I had to wash the dishes and get our son ready for bed. About 1:30 my wife's thrashing woke me up. I got up to get a glass of water. Good thing I did, our son's bear was pressed up against the fireplace. The bear was too hot to touch. Left alone, it would have caught fire within minutes. Good thing I got up for a glass of water.

Night two:

My Version: 'We wish you a merry Christmas, we wish you a merry Christmas....and a happy new year...'

The song drifted through my dreams, and it wasn't until the last strains had died away that I realized it was our doorbell. I sat up, groggy and disoriented. My husband was rubbing his eyes too. We looked at each other and glanced at the clock 1:58 a.m. Suddenly we realize our doorbell just rang at 2 in the morning.

"Go answer the door!" my husband whispered loudly.

"No, way! That's your job." I hissed back, fumbling in our dark room for my robe.

"Someone may have hit an animal," he argued back.

Hitting an animal was the last thing my brain was envisioning. Maybe I read to many crime novels, but my first thought was to get a gun—not a shovel.

I crept over to the window. There was a 20-something-man standing on our porch with a gas can, and there's a U-haul van parked in our driveway.

By now my husband is finally answering the door. I hung

back in the shadows.

The man said he'd run out of gas and just needed to fill up his can. Holding up new, red gas jug to emphasize his dilemma.

"I'm sorry," my husband said, "we don't have any here." The man kept repeating his question and waving around the can, getting more agitated by the second.

I had my finger on the 9 button on my cell phone, and was just starting to push it, when our Hound decided he'd had enough. He set up an angry raucous, and quickly the young man left, muttering in Spanish.

He hadn't quite reached the U-haul van when the lights turned on and the engine started. He got into the passenger side and it drove out our driveway—and turned right—away from town and any gas stations.

By now, both our dogs were worked up, and they spent the rest of the night storming around the perimeter and barking.

Meanwhile I laid awake for hours wondering what they were really up to? Who drives a U-haul around in the middle of the night? Who wakes someone up if you aren't entirely out of gas? Who happens to have a gas can when they do actually run out of fuel?

His Version: The doorbell rang around 2 a.m. My wife woke up first, but she was too twitterpated to go answer it. Some 20-year-old-punk driving a U-haul wanted gas. Suspicious, since he drove all the way up our driveway. He was getting worked up until the Hound decided to intimidate. They drove away in their U-haul that was out of fuel, and in the opposite direction of fuel. After a quick call to the police to report it, I got a glass of water and headed to bed, grumbling I missed an important hour of sleep.

Grandpa's Ivy League Education

*N*early everyone in this country is concerned with getting a good education. Going to the right schools, taking the right classes and getting high grades. Hours are spent sending out applications, studying for SATs, and visiting campuses trying to decide what school, college, or university will provide you or your child the best education possible.

But some of the best lessons I ever learned had nothing to do with scholastics, and everything to do with my Grandpa.

Grandpa Johnny loved teaching small children about hygiene. He taught his grandchildren and their friends, his great-grandchildren and their friends, and I'm sure many, many others. I was probably 4 or 5 when he traumatized—er—I mean taught me my first lesson. He called me over real close, then whipped out his teeth with amazing speed and dexterity! I was traumatized, Grandpa was amused, and my parents never had to fuss to get me to brush my teeth after that. They'd just say "only brush the ones you want to keep." Hygiene lesson learned.

Grandpa taught us about sleeping habits. This was one lesson I wasn't so keen on learning. He thought nothing of getting up before the crack of dawn to start on chores...and if truth be told...I didn't think much of it either!

He and I both agreed the morning was the best part of the day—we just disagreed on where we should spend it. He and my sister would rise bright-eyed and bushy-tailed, and I would drag myself out of bed, minutes before school started. That's when I learned that in my Grandparent's house there are no such things as *Sleeping Beauties.* In their house, they are *Lay-a-bed-Uglies.*

Grandpa was a clock watcher. Lunch was at noon, along with Luke and Laura (General Hospital) and later Perry Mason. Quitting time was 4. Chores at 5. And bedtime was at 9 p.m. Sharp. "It's 9 o'clock, you'll turn into a pumpkin," he'd say, shutting off the TV or lights, or whatever switch he was close to as he quickly headed to bed. My grandma would wait until the bedroom door shut, and on went both the TV and lights. That's when I learned another, albeit more subtle lesson: the rooster may rule the roost, but who rules the rooster?

Grandpa also taught the days of the week. This was another lesson that didn't fall on receptive ears. Those ears belonging to my grandmother on the other side of the family. I am not sure how the original discussion came about, but what resulted was a decade-long dispute over the Lord's Day. Grandma Edith believing it to be Saturday, and Grandpa Johnny doing as much as he could to convince her it was on Sunday.

The more flustered she became, the more Grandpa Johnny would tease her. He would get her so riled up, she could only swat at him. If there was ever a lull in the conversation and Grandma Edith was within hearing distance, you can be sure that Grandpa would ask her about the Lord's Day.

But Grandpa wasn't always a giant tease, sometimes he was extraordinarily polite—occasionally to his own detriment. Grandpa taught us that exaggeration, even at it's finest can really choke a person. Grandpa during some of his earlier years, ate dinner at a potluck after church. Taking a rather large bite of pie, he found he was having trouble trying to swallowed it. Terrible didn't even seem to describe it. It was sitting in a big lump on his tongue when the baker of the pie asked him how he was enjoying it.

"And Grandpa laid it on thick," his wife recalled. "He just wouldn't shut up," she laughed at the memory. "Grandpa told her many times and in many ways just how great a pie she had made." A few weeks later, the lady baker, presented him with a whole pie just like it to take home—because he had loved hers so much. Grandma Betty, (his wife) gleefully recalled serving it to him, feeling his exaggeration had earned him his "just desserts."

Grandpa Johnny also taught his daughters about anatomy. Specifically how the foot-bone is connected to the voice box. One afternoon while building fence, Grandpa Johnny and his daughters were loaded up in their Jeep.

His dad, Grandpa Rayl was getting ready to come too. For whatever reason, Grandpa Rayl wouldn't ride with both feet in the vehicle, preferring to have one leg out and the door ajar. This particular day, was no different. They had stopped and Grandpa Rayl was standing against the jeep, one foot in and one foot out.

It was at that moment Grandpa Johnny decided it was time to go. He drove over his dad's foot. Grandpa Rayl, without moving, started hollering and swearing. Grandpa

Johnny put the Jeep into reverse and backed back over his foot, to see what was wrong with his dad. As the swearing increased in volume, it was easy for the girls to see the direct correlation between the foot bone and the voice box.

Grandpa also taught us how to play games. Grandpa was competitive—with anything: basketball, chess, ping pong, and Scrabble. It didn't really matter what he was playing, Grandpa was in it to win it.

"Sucker's lead!" he would holler when you found yourself losing to him. And if the playing field started to even out he would try psyching you out with "your palms are getting sweaty."

Once during a most heated game of Scrabble with his daughter, I think his own hands must have gotten sweaty. Sweaty enough the gameboard crashed to the floor and the game was left unfinished without a victor.

I'm not sure I got his competitive gene, but I am thankful Grandpa taught all of us to be such good losers. I mean, not that we really ever lose...it's really just a friendly game... there are no winners or losers...but if we ever really *wanted* to, we would clean their clocks...IF we really wanted to.

Grandpa also taught us about the consequences of being stubborn. One afternoon dinner consisted of potato soup and crackers. Everyone dished up and Grandpa dug in. A bottle of cayenne pepper sat on the table. The bottle was passed around, and for reasons unknown—whether intentional or accidental, my grandpa poured several tablespoons onto his soup. When she'd seen what he'd done, my mom offered to get him a new bowl, or at least scrape some of it out. But he insisted he liked it like that. We all laughed. And Grandma told him to dump it out. But he assured us it was nothing and he'd be fine. The more we laughed, the more adamant he became that he would eat it *and like it*!

He started in, and we all watched in awe. His face got red and sweaty, his nose swollen, his handkerchief damp, and he refilled his milk glass repeatedly until the gallon jug was empty. But to his credit. he ate the whole bowl. In spicy, sweaty, stubborn silence.

Grandpa also taught us about Candy. As children we loved going to parades and collecting the few stray pieces of candy that fell our way. It wasn't until I was an adult that I learned I was doing it all wrong. Grandpa showed us how to collect candy at parades. You have to be an active participant. Sitting alongside the street will merit you a handful of tootsie rolls at best, so if you want candy (which is the primary reason of attending parades) you must first bring a hat. Then wear a bright shirt, and it helps if you wear your neon pink "tenny runners," (Grandpa's word for tennis shoes.) Anything to gather attention. Then when a person in the parade glances your way, you holler loudly "Bet you can't hit my hat!"

Nearly everyone takes the bait and tosses a few pieces. Most missing by a good distance. Then, most people, surprised at how bad their aim was, try a second and sometimes a third time. By this time, other people on the float are getting in on the act. Candy comes raining down in all directions: star bursts, suckers, jaw breakers, and even a box or two of nerds. And before the first parade entry has passed, you have collected more candy that the last two parades you have attended combined!

Grandpa Johnny also taught us about gambling. It probably wouldn't help us in a trip to Las Vegas, but he familiarized us with the concept of betting. Grandpa loved betting on things. He bet we couldn't build something, or climb something. He bet us we couldn't beat him at Jeopardy. He bet us we couldn't do certain tasks within a time limit. You name it and Grandpa bet on it. And his favorite reward to bet with? A milkshake. It's a good thing he didn't take betting very serious though, because *I'm willing to bet* that not many of us that won those bets *ever* ended up eating ice cream.

There have been so many lessons over the years, but perhaps the most lessons were taught at Easter

Ordinary families dye eggs for the kids, hide eggs for the kids, and get Easter baskets for the kids. But we have already established that my family is far from ordinary.

This was the day of Grandpa Johnny's $100 egg hunt. A rarely found egg. An egg that legends are made of, and stories are written about. The actual $100 matters less than holding the title as finder…the first family member to find it, still has the check in her bureau, and swears she'd have to be starving before she'd cash it.

Past hiding places include being buried in the ground under some used tires; drilled inside a fencepost, tied to an anchor and thrown into the feeder canal; stuffed inside a yellow wasp trap; inside the heating coils of the water trough, and inside the hubcaps of the stocktrailer. And this list is far from inclusive. The few times it has been found, Grandpa's face waffled somewhere between admiration and despair (he wasn't a big fan of giving out cash).

This is not an egg hunt for the faint or weak of heart, I've seen family members scour the dumpster and the feed bins, climb the barn roof and wiggle around under the foundation of the house. They've tilled the strawberry beds, pushed big bales off the feed trucks, and removed parts off of machinery. I've seen adults climb trees, move irrigation pipe, shake out wasp traps, stick their hands in buckets of old grease, and turn over cow pies.

Through Easter, Grandpa has taught us to bury our money, to change the rules if we don't like them and to laugh together.

That $100 egg has made for cheap family therapy. The family comes together, and we laugh and share while we dye the eggs; we push and shove while we hunt the eggs; and later we reminisce and tell egg tales (our family's version of fish tales).

Photos albums will show 4 generations of dirt-smeared, grease-stained kids and adults picking twigs out of their hair and dusting insulation off their jeans after a rigorous egg hunt.

Forget ordinary, this crazy family is extraordinary… I thank God for dentures and Grandpa's impossible egg hunts. Those quirky memories will provide a way to hold on to the things we love, the things we are, the things we never want to lose, without quite so much pain.

Wiped Out

There I was, standing in the toilet paper aisle in the middle of the night. It had been one of those weeks that felt like a series of tasks you absolutely must get done before they don't matter anymore.

The 10-day forecast had called for rain, which meant that everything took second-fiddle to getting the hay up. *Breakfast?* I'm sure there's an old bag of peanuts in the tractor. *Sleep?* Remind me what that is after first cutting is tarped or sold. *Laundry?* A good shake ought to get most of the dirt from your pockets and cuffs. *Toilet paper?* Uh oh, Houston. We have a problem...

All my life, I've heard, "You don't know what you have until it's gone," well, that is definitely true when it comes to toilet paper! With the weather forecast continuing to predict gloomy rain, I opted to "borrow" the tp from the shop bathroom, rather than waste valuable tractor-time for a shopping trip. That seemed like a great plan—until the shop bathroom ran out also.

Thankfully, my husband keeps an emergency roll in the

harrowbed. Unfortunately, it wasn't a full one. The people who calculate such things, have determined that the average American uses 57 sheets of toilet paper each day, 8.6 sheets per visit. At that rate, the sad little emergency roll wouldn't buy us much time.

But the threat of that rainstorm looming in the forecast, pushed toilet paper to the far back of our minds, and we continued pressing on to get that hay up green and dry. Coffee, Mountain Dew, and sheer determination kept us at it as the nights grew even shorter—but not as short as a roll of toilet paper in the house. Just like our week, it kept going faster and faster until it ended with unfortunate timing.

According to a Cottonell poll, 72% of people prefer to hang toilet paper with the first sheet over the roll and 28% prefer the first sheet under the roll. I am a "sheet over" kind of girl, but at that moment, I wouldn't have complained about a roll perched precariously on top of the holder. Luckily, my son remembered another partial roll in one of our snowmobiles.

The week's work sped on, as did the remaining rolls of tp. I remembered with nostalgia the years of large Sears catalogs. Using tp with page numbers might seem redneck to some, but during a ridiculously busy week of harvest, I think it was just old-fashioned genius.

The night finally arrived when even MacGyver would have come up empty. That's how I found myself staring at an aisle of toilet paper at midnight.

I usually buy my toilet paper at Costco, where my choices are limited to a handful of brands—making it easy to compare prices. Perhaps it was the late hour, or perhaps the lack of sleep, but somehow standing there, those toilet paper packages seemed especially confusing. How can a person calculate which package is a better deal when a roll isn't a roll. Some packages boasted "mega-rolls," "jumbo-rolls," and "1,000 sheet rolls." Others more simply stated that

12=48, and 36=72.

It was obvious I was not going to be able to compare rolls to price shop, but maybe I could calculate it based on the number of sheets. A quick glance at the packages revealed that the number of sheets on various "double-rolls" ranged from 176-352. Lest one spend time calculating the cost per sheet, it is prudent to note that the sheet size can vary between brands by nearly an inch!

I looked around at the packages, all vying to end up in my cart. My brain felt muddled. I stood nearly comatose as the little squirrel in my brain tried to coax the wheel into spinning.

I was just reaching for one package that said 12=48, when I noticed the package beside it boasting 12=54. "What kind of math is this?" the price-shopping part of my brain screamed. That's when I noticed the single rolls of toilet paper. I may not understand the math behind the cost of toilet paper, but I am really confused with buying a single roll. I may not be able to easily find the better bargain between the 12-pack and the 30-pack, but a single roll?...I mean, really, are you trying to quit?

With my brain still muddling through the murky math of double-rolls, I grabbed the big package with the purple...because I liked the color.

As the cashier rang me up, I decided that buying toilet paper ranked as my second favorite domestic duty, falling only slightly behind airing out my husband's work boots, all the while holding my breath until I pass out from lack of fresh air.

Raining on the Wicked Witch

"*E*ighty-two degrees with a 12% chance of rain and 4 mph wind" read the weather forecast. "Better count on a cold, rainy, windy weekend," I told my husband.

He double checked the statistics. "It looks like it'll be nice."

"Well I say it's going to rain—might even have a thunderstorm."

"Look." He held out his phone so I could see the forecast myself. He was right. It looked like lovely weather. But we had cut hay this week, and we had a camping trip coming up. A camping trip that would include tents.

"—and we all know that rain clouds will go hundreds of miles out of their way to drizzle on tent canvas."

My husband rolled his eyes, after all, he was looking right at a lovely weekend weather forecast.

"I know what it says...but...we could make a sign that reads: 'hay cut—check. Hay raked—check. Hay dried—check. Baler ready—check. It's raining.'"

I know that the weather is based upon satellites, weather

patterns, barometric pressure and lots of computer models and statistics, but sometimes I think the rheumatism in Granny's bones was almost as accurate.

If I was to create a weather prediction technology, it would take the information gleaned from the computer, add in some arthritis and maybe a little rheumatism along with the following daily questionnaire:

1. Will you or your neighbor be washing your car or patio today?

2. Will you or your neighbor be cutting hay any time in the next week?

3. Is there a scout group going camping in the next week?

For each yes answer calculate an additional 33% chance of rain, for each maybe answer add 15%. If you answer yes to all three, then you best test your lightning rods, and make sure your hail canons are working.

We checked the weather periodically as the days got closer. Each time the numbers were a bit lower, but it still wasn't forecasting rain. I was hopeful—but not optimistic. Less than a week before the camping trip, with many acres of hay on the ground, Granny's rheumatism seemed to be acting up. The animals were agitated, and the morning air felt heavy.

The smell of rain drifted off and on throughout the day. By evening the sky looked a bit dark, and I wasn't surprised to see big rain drops making patterns on the dirty windshield. Then came the thunder and lightning and loss of electricity.

The dog paced back and forth, the hot tub lid went crashing across the yard, the neighbor's sheep shelter went visiting the adjoining pasture, some of the pretty rows of hay also went visiting and what didn't got a good bath. It wasn't a twister by any form of the imagination, but as branches scraped the windows, I couldn't help but think of Kansas' own Dorothy and our upcoming camping trip.

For the first time ever I felt a touch of sympathy for the Wicked Witch of the West. She probably never experienced the joy of camping: campfires, guitars, hikes, roasted hot dogs and s'mores... Which meant she also never experienced hiking blisters, ticks, aching bones from sleeping on unlevel rocky ground—and of course the rain. Rain which causes wet tents, wet sleeping bags, wet dogs, and wet socks.

One last glance at the weather forecast showed the highs plunging lower, and the precipitation percentages increasing. I looked down at my fingers holding the phone. Did I see just the slightest tint of green? I think I'm coming down with witchitis. It's probably just a matter of time before it covers my whole body!

Perhaps I'll skip the rainy camping trip, I'm feeling the need for a pair of powerful, red shoes—something *worth* melting for!

Up a Creek with Half a Paddle

*T*hree-fourths of the Earth's surface is water and only one-fourth is land. Seems like a pretty strong indication that we were intended to spend triple the amount of time in a boat than on a tractor.

Everyone has their vices, and it's no secret that I'm an *aqua*holic; I love water. No matter what the problem, I think the solution always involves water—whether it is sweat, tears, the ocean, or a good watermelon. If there is magic on this planet, it's in water and children. Not to be confused with children in kayaks in water. But I'm getting ahead of myself.

The morning had arrived bright and sunny. Snacks and drinks were carefully packed into bags, while we donned hats, life-jackets, water shoes and loaded up eight kayaks—ready for adventure. For years I had wanted to kayak this particular stretch of river—and today was the day!

My excitement was tempered only by a distant memory of floating down a river on innertubes during my teen years. It also had started as a sunny day. It ended near midnight—

hungry, cold, and covered in stinging nettle scratches. We had torn nails, lost sandals, and my vehicle had been vandalized while it sat waiting for our return. Even the police were out looking for us.

This was a different river, with a different group of people, and we were on kayaks instead of innertubes...but I still couldn't shake the feeling that this may be another learning trip.

"This is awesome!" my 9-year-old and his friend shouted to each other as they maneuvered through the first set of small rapids. We all seemed to agree, even the 11-week-old puppy that balanced precariously off the front of a kayak.

After an hour, the swift rapids gave way to a gentle current. The scenery was gorgeous, so no one seemed to mind the leisurely pace. After another few hours however, the river got deeper and even more idle—which also meant harder paddling.

My 2-year-old, sitting in front of me found this slow pace boring, and the end was nowhere in sight. As the blazing sun moved slowly across the sky, the other kids (while not exactly complaining), began letting us know of aching backs and blistered hands and empty stomachs. I have to admit the underside of me felt pretty uncomfortable as well.

My 2-year-old was getting tired, and his life-jacket was irritating his chin. "Look at the fisherman," I would say, trying to distract him. He glanced toward the shore, but within moments was pulling at his jacket again.

"Oh! Look at the splash that big fish made!" I pointed toward ripples in the river. I kept trying to interest him in our surroundings, but he wasn't interested. He had found a new past time. "Helping" me paddle—first with his arms, and then his legs. Paddling a kayak is exercise on a good day, but rowing while a 2-year-old is wrapped around your paddle is quite the *'oar-deal.'* Obviously, he's not a believer in the *"paddle solo, sleep tandem"* rule. I kept *trying* to paddle and he kept *trying* to help—until I got the bright idea to split my oar so each of us could row.

Thrilled to have his very own oar, he began paddling on the left. Surprisingly, not only was the oar entertaining him, but he was doing a pretty decent job of propelling that side of the kayak.

At first, I watched him like a hawk, to make sure he didn't drop it in the ever-deepening river. Minutes passed, and we had picked up a nice rhythm together and soon had resumed our position in the front of our group. Before long, I was lost in conversation with the other mom in our group.

"Oops, Mommy!"

I glanced down to see a fleeting glimpse of white as the oar vanished in the murky river. Multiple diving attempts brought up nothing but large sticks. It was a painful moment when we finally admitted defeat—and it didn't take long to realize that half the paddle makes twice the paddler.

We did eventually make it to our destination, but it wasn't quick. The only quick thing that happens with half an oar, is exchanging your position in the lead, for one in the far back.

I think my 2-year-old must have known we were in a predicament because he seemed pretty content to play with sticks the rest of the afternoon. As the river lazily threaded its way through the hills, the trees, and the fishermen, I had to work twice as hard to keep up, which gave me much time to think about my actions. I decided it is more prudent to take a conservative course of action, even if it means a baby cries, than it is to engage in risky behavior which you may regret later when it is both the baby *and* your muscles crying—or as my husband said, "Better safe with one oar than sorry with a half."

When we finally pulled our kayaks out of the water—tired, hungry and sore—I tossed my half-paddle into the back of the pickup and decided there really is merit to the saying: Love many, trust a few...but *always* paddle your own canoe!

I've Got Ewe Babe....
Me and Ewe...

"*H*ow do you feel about bummer lambs?"
"Um, no."
"What do you mean no? They are so cute?"
"I would love to, but unfortunately...no!"
"But they are free."
"There are worse things I could agree to, I just can't think of any at the moment."
"Your Grandpa is getting some..."
"Let him get some then. But on a scale of maybe to absolutely, I say absolutely *not* for us! Do you know how much work sheep can be?"

My newly-wedded husband and I continued this conversation for a few more minutes, before I went back to work, and he went back to look at the "cute, adorable baby lambs" with my Grandpa.

Girls often have the reputation for being vague and expecting their spouses to read between the lines; but when I hung up the phone that afternoon, I felt I had been overly clear with my opinion—that is until I arrived home and discovered eight bummer lambs snuggled under a heat-lamp in the barn.

That's when I realized something all too relevant with human interactions—You may believe you understand what you think someone has said, but what you don't realize, is that what you heard is not what they meant.

My husband also learned something important—no matter how much I say no, once an animal (no matter how scraggly), is on my property, I don't have the heart to turn it out.

At first I grumbled as I put on my boots to do middle-of-the-night feedings—but soon those scraggly animals won me over—and I forgave my husband for expecting his opinion to come out of my mouth, and my Grandpa for taking my animal-loving husband to a sheep farm.

That was 13 years —and many, many scraggly animals ago.

Those original eight lambs quickly multiplied and soon our pasture was filled with sheep. One of those original bummers, "Dirty Harry," gave birth the following year to a waspy set of twins. We kept the ewe-lamb and named her "Junior." She could jump out of anything—we should have given her a middle name, just so she could have understood more clearly how much trouble she was in from incident to incident.

As the herd grew, so did the rest of our lives: farming, community, a family of our own—and it wasn't long before our sheep became numbers on an ear tag instead of pet names. Except for Junior. She was one of a kind. She would come nuzzle for crackers, then abruptly turn and jump over the fence. She was wild and gentle; unpredictably predictable. She was a good mix of her calm mother, and her angry father who had once jumped the fence and dented a visitor's car door.

It was with a sad heart when I found that my dear old girl had gone to greener pastures. She marked the end of an era.

She was from a time before kids, a time when my husband and I were still learning about marriage and communication. Not to imply that we have graduated those courses, but we definitely understand each other better that we did that first year of marriage.

Just recently I was looking at buying a couple of mini-goats. My husband saw some of the photos I'd been looking at online. He didn't say "no." I think his response was something like "I'd rather jump in a lake of piranhas!"

I'm thinking about naming the smaller of the two goats "Junior Jr."

Racing Through VBS

To be sure of hitting the target, shoot first and wherever you hit, call it the target. That has seemed to be my mantra this last week. I love Vacation Bible School. My husband and I have been VBS leaders for 9 years now and we usually love it. Creating the program, designing the craft, finding tangible daily demonstrations—the only thing that would make it better would be if they scheduled it in the winter! Sometimes I think VBS actually stands for Very Busy Season.

Jotting down ideas from the swather cab, lining up helpers from the semi truck, organizing the demonstrations from the tractor, it was finally planned out—or perhaps I should say the bulls-eye was set up, but we weren't going to be too hasty about calling it the target yet.

Our theme was "Racing from Egypt to Canaan," exploring the many "pit stops" the Israelites had along the way. To help set the scene, we used a semi-load of straw bales to create Mount Sinai and the walls of Jericho. For the Red Sea we made a straw pool lined with black plastic—I couldn't decide if Moses would have been proud or appalled. With our background completed, it was time to focus on the stage area. Bringing the racing theme to the forefront, we set up racing slicks, checkered flags, a side-by-side, four-wheelers and dirtbikes—both in adult and youth sizes.

To complete our program, the kids' craft would be to build a soap box car. T minus 5 days, the bulls-eye was set up, the gun leveled—but just before the trigger was squeezed, our music crew had a family emergency and cancelled.

Days of frantic scrambling paid off, and now our sights were readjusted to the new target. The scope was double-checked—just to be sure. A deep breath in, the trigger finger tightened—and our first night time demonstration bailed—just hours before the program was to start. My husband scrolled diligently through his phone trying to find a Plan B, or Plan C, or even Plan O. But at 5:55 and a few seconds—our program starting at 6, we just closed our eyes and pulled the trigger...the target being whatever we hit.

With no racing device to show the expecting kids, we did what any farmer would do—we brought out floor jacks, impact drivers and tire irons and let the kids pretend they were in "the pits" changing tires. All except the really little kids, who just took rides up and down on the jacks.

As the week progressed, our target seemed to readjust daily. Horse rides turned into horse-powered atv rides, group leaders changed faces as people either got sick or headed off to attend weddings.

Part way through the week, a cousin from central Oregon brought her five kids to come, stay, and attend the craziness. We discovered real quick how different a family of four is, versus a family of seven.

First off, I don't have enough dishes.

Secondly, I should buy more plastic cups and less glass ones, and third, when you have a large family, meals are much more of a production. I'm no Julia Child in the kitchen

—yet I've never felt as bumbling as Mrs. Doubtfire. We'll eat throughout the day as hunger strikes, although if I was completely honest, I must say that I usually think about food after someone's stomach begins growling.

Our house functions best as a Do It Yourself Bed and Breakfast. I discovered though, that a family of seven requires a bit more planning. It seemed that no sooner had the last breakfast dish been washed and put away, than my cousin was planning lunch, and then supper—although I am sure there must have been time in between.

My cousin is a great planner when it comes to meals. I, on the other hand, will look in the cupboards, pull out some random ingredients and food is served. All I really need is cheese and/or black pepper—that's practically like duct tape and baler twine in my kitchen—they can fix anything. My cousin gave me a couple of *looks*, that my self-consciousness took to mean "what kind of grandmother will you make if you don't enjoy cooking?"

As VBS wore on, we sang songs, built our soap box cars, got to climb in race cars, pretend to be horses as we ran through the barrels, and watch motocross racers. On Sunday, our VBS finale, we set up a track to race the cars we had worked all week to build. There were tunnels, hair-pin curves, and corners lined with tires.

I felt that we had shot a pretty decent target after all—even if it wasn't what we had been aiming for in the original sight. Just then, a friend steps up and pats my shoulder. "I don't know how you come up with these ideas—it's amazing." My cousin's face flashed before my eyes, looking at me with despair at my lack of meal planning skill.

I smiled at my friend, "Well, I will be the grandmother that provides crafts and activities, but asks her grandkids to bring the food!"

It's a Ladder Kind of Day

It was one of those "I walked under a ladder" kind of days. I had slept fitfully throughout the night, only sleeping real sound right before my alarm blasted my morning into full swing. Unfortunately though, I had set it for the wrong time.

I scrambled through my morning routine, poured a bowl of cereal and was just about to add milk when I noticed it was fat-free, lactose-free. Ugh. I put it back in the fridge, and turned on the tea pot instead. I pulled out a tea bag and stuck it in my thermos as I headed out the door. Slid behind the wheel of my pickup and took a deep breath...and a sip of tea. It was terribly bitter. I looked at the tag. It was some kind of medicated sore throat tea. Yuck.

I looked at the clock, too late to remedy my mistake. Once on the road, I began a mental checklist of what I needed... and realized I had the camera, but no SD card for it.

The day was just getting started: my pen didn't write, the pickup was low on fuel, I only had 2.27 cents in change in my wallet, and the check engine light came on during my drive to work. By then, all parts of my body were rejecting the nasty tea, and I found myself in dire need of a bathroom.

The last few miles seemed to stretch on, and it seemed an eternity until I was heading down the hall, my sights zeroed in on the women's bathroom. My relief was short lived as it smelled as if it had been out of order all week. I hesitated only slightly as I entered the men's bathroom next door... and that was only because it took a second to find the light switch.

At my desk, things didn't improve. Gremlins seemed to be partying in my computer, and my computer seemed to glitch in time to their disco ball. My sister surprised me with lunch, and I thought my day must be turning around. She handed me a luscious looking orange. I reached for my knife and realized I'd left it on my dresser. She handed me hers, and I quickly sliced the peel. I tried to pull it apart, and squirted orange juice everywhere. It wouldn't peel. I had pieces of orange all over my desk. It was a mess. You'd have thought I'd never peeled an orange before.

The day continued on like that, I tripped over the dog bowl, I sat down and my chair nearly rolled out from under me, and the gremlins continued the party in my computer.

As I drove home, a police car pulled in behind me. My hands immediately went to 10 and 2, and I suddenly realized my license expires the end of the month. I have no recollection what was playing on the radio, I have no idea how many people passed me, but I was acutely aware of centering myself between the two lines and not exceeding the speed limit.

I finally arrived back at home, ready to complain of my "walking under a ladder" kind of day. I was greeted at the door by the smell of homemade soup, and my little boy on the counter putting candles in a cake.

"We made a cake for your Happy Birthday, Momma," he sang out. He proudly showed me his cake and frosting job. Happy birthday was sung, and the cake was cut. It had a strong baking soda taste, and the frosting was kind of scarce. He smiled so proudly, and I think it was the best birthday cake I ever ate.

Then he gave me a box he'd wrapped himself. To: Momma, Love Keagan, it said. Inside was one of the ugliest sweatshirts to bear WSU's logo. He said "I didn't like it, but I thought you would." I hugged him so tight.

Next time I feel like I'm having one of those kind of days, I'm going to remind myself that sometimes you may have to walk under a ladder before you can climb its rungs.

The Funny Smells

You know you're living the farm life, when you line up in front of the air compressor to "clean up" before running into town.

The Little Half Moon

"*T*urn left at the blue canoe," my husband instructed.

"What is a 'blue canoe,' asked the young girl who was riding with me.

I laughed, "just a funny way of referring to those little blue outhouses."

She wrinkled her nose, "ewwww, I hate those things. I think it's gross to use toilets that don't flush." She continued on that line of conversation, I snuck a glance at her as she was cheerily rattling on about some friends she knew that have even gone outside before.

It reminded me of a few years ago when we took a group of teenagers to the sand dunes for an afternoon of adventure on four-wheelers. Everyone was having a good time.... until one of the young ladies needed to use the facilities.... of which there were none. I'd never thought it too big a problem before, it was only a short ride out to the sage brush and brambles where there were many spots for a lady needing her privacy.

She looked dubious, but she followed me out to the

pucker brush. I pointed off one way direction for her, and I headed the other way, no need to waste a trip. I returned to my four-wheeler and waited...and waited...and waited. I didn't have a watch, but I'm sure more than 10 minutes had passed. Finally I shouted, "you didn't tell me you had to do more than pee!"

"I don't" she yelled back.

"Well what's taking so long? Are you okay?"

"I'm fine," she answered, "I just can't pee outside."

She came walking back, looking pained. She didn't ride much longer, before she had to leave the dunes and find a gas station bathroom.

"What are you smiling at?" the girl in my pickup asked, bringing me back to the present.

I shook my head, "just listening" I said giving her my best attempt at a wink.

"So I was saying," she continued, "that someone just bought the house next to my Grandpa's place. It's a cabin. Someone must have taken out the electricity, because there is no microwave or X-box or anything. And they don't even have water or even toilets. I don't know when they are going to put them in. Maybe it'll be like in olden times where they had to use an outhouse. Wouldn't that be scary going outside to go to the bathroom. What would you do at night time?"

Wow. I was feeling old. I know outhouses weren't terribly common in my childhood. But I've used my share, and know the difference between a one-holer and two. I remember listening to stories my parents and grandparents shared about outhouse tipping while occupied. Yes, I find bathrooms more convenient as well, yet it surprised me to hear how "scary" it would be to "go outside."

It made me want to play "Ode to the Little Brown Shack Out Back." Unfortunately it was on cassette tape, which would have probably brought up a whole other topic of "old" and "scary." So instead I hummed the words to myself and thanked my lucky stars I grew up when and where I did.

Ode to the Little Brown Shack Out Back

They passed an ordinance in the town
they said we'd have to tear it down
That little old shack out back so dear to me
Though the health department said
it's day was over and dead
It will stand forever in my memory

It was not so long ago
that I went tripping through the snow
Out to that house behind my old hound dog
Where I would sit me down to rest
like a snowbird on his nest
And I'd read that Sears and Roebuck catalog

Oh I would hum a happy tune
peeping through the quarter moon
As my daddy's kin had done so much before
It was in that quiet spot daily cares could be forgot
And it gave the same relief to rich and poor

Now it was not a castle fair
but I could dream my future there
Build my castle to the yellow jackets drone
I could orbit round the sun
fight with General Washington
Or be a king upon a golden throne

It wasn't fancy built at all
we had newspapers on the wall
It was air-conditioned in the wintertime
Oh it was just an humble hut
but it's door was never shut
And a man could get inside without a dime

Don't let them tear that little brown building down
There's not another like it in the country or the town

Men and their Crazy "Two Canoe" Ideas

"The more things change, the more they stay the same." I couldn't help but think of the epigram of Jean-Baptiste Alphonse Karr while reading with my son one afternoon. Snuggled together in a hammock, we were enjoying an almost warm spring-like afternoon—the kind that Mother Nature has been extremely stingy with this year.

The blue sky overhead was dotted with white puffy, cotton-ball clouds, the breeze wafted the fruit tree blossoms scent deliciously over our noses, and our dogs were snoozing contentedly under the hammock—my pyranese on one side, my son's blood hound on the other. It was one of those perfect moments that one wants to imprint on your mind's eye. I leaned a little closer, and closed my eyes, listening to my son's voice as he read aloud.

The story was one of a young boy and his family traveling from Tennessee to Texas in 1852. The challenges they faced often made my son stop and wonder. Why would they conserve gun powder…couldn't they just buy more? Why did they eat everything they shot…even when it was gristly, fatty meat like raccon? Why didn't they heat up the water after every person took a bath? What was a flint and why didn't they just use matches? In these ways, the story seemed far removed from us—that is until they got to a crossing at St Francis River.

There was a ferry to take the wagons across. People were swimming children and animals across. There was also a trapper who was taking people across in his canoe. As he was charging much less, he was doing much more business than the ferry driver.

"Too bad you can't haul wagons in them canoes," said one man from Kentucky.

"Who says I can't?" the trapper replied.

And so it was that while the wife protested, the man from Kentucky made a deal with the trapper to take his canoe for less than half of what the ferryman was charging. Two canoes were lashed to the wagon—and somehow they managed to get one under the left set of wheels, and the other under the right—then the wagon started across the river.

The ferryman, having just lost a three-dollar fare, started stomping on his hat and cursing, while the rest of the people stared in amazement and laughter at the wagon crossing the river on two canoes. About halfway across, the canoes seemed to go down a hair in front. Then in the back.

"Paddle faster," the Kentucky man pleaded.

But it was to no avail. A full thirty feet from the shore, water poured over the sides of a those canoes, and they sank like rocks. The trapper began swimming for his life—not afraid of drowning, but powerfully alarmed at the rifle the wife of the Kentucky man was aiming in his direction.

It was at this, that my son could no longer contain his laughter. He let the book fall to his chest as he laughed and coughed and snorted. "What a silly thing to do," he giggled. "All to save two dollars. Couldn't he tell it was a bad idea?"

My grandmother used to say about a particular romance

author "They just change outfits and mansions..." My son looked up at me, still laughing, "I knew it was a bad idea, why didn't they?"

"Well, my son...someday you will understand—it's a guy thing. And most wives will be able to relate to the rifle-armed lady on the shore." He looked at me with confusion. I began telling him a story that happened when he was just a year old.

My husband and I had flown back east to drive home two pickups. My husband rented a trailer and we were planning on driving one and hauling the other. But to save a few bucks he rented the "one-dollar canoe." The trailer wasn't long enough or wide enough so he used boards, and ramps, a hi-lift jack and a lot of ratchets to get the pickup on it. When it was finally on, it looked precariously like I imagine that wagon did on those two canoes. We drove just a few painful miles—that trailer fishtailing like crazy—I didn't know if I should be more afraid for us, the cars passing us, or the pickup whose back tires were overhanging the trailer on long boards. I could empathize with Kentuckian's wife. I wished I would have had a rifle!

"So what happened?" my son asked.

"Thankfully we stopped before the "canoes" sank. Then you and I drove one pickup home, and Daddy drove the other along with his cheap trailer. The moral of the story is that shortcuts don't often work out in the long run."

"Maybe not," he grinned, "but they sure are funnier to talk about."

Pete the Parrot

Some people are just born funny. My dad's caveat to that is "funny looking, funny smelling, funny sounding." My brother-in-law is funny and often funny in all of these categories. Joe is quite the character: 6 foot 7, skinny as a rail, and always full of borderline-ill-advised adventures. Such was the case one Saturday afternoon. Joe recalls it this way...

My buddies John, James and I were bored so we headed off to the beach to go biking—the scenery there was always good on a sunny day. John and James took their mountain bikes and I brought an old beach cruiser I had purchased at a yard sale for a few bucks. If I had to describe the bike today, I would say it was quite hideous, but back then I thought it was the coolest thing around.

I added to its flare by installing a parrot, who I named Pete, onto the enormous handlebars. Pete was a squeaky toy I used to warn unsuspecting pedestrians that I was about to pass them. The bike also sported a seat large enough to be confused with a mattress from a child's crib.

We arrived at Newport Beach in board shorts, Hawaiian shirts, straw hats and flip flops. We unloaded the bikes out of the back of my Jeep and started riding down the boardwalk.

Pete was having a good time squeaking at pedestrians as I huffed past them on my way to nowhere. We eventually got bored and began looking for something else to do. We decided to ride up to the top of a hill that overlooked the ocean.

This turned out to be quite a workout since my bike only had one speed and with the enormous handlebars was nearly impossible to stand up and peddle. I eventually made it to the top and was rewarded with great views and a snow cone—mostly the snow cone.

We decided to head back down the hill and get some dinner. John and James took off first. Not wanting to be last, I decided it was necessary to pass them—which involved getting on the sidewalk as there wasn't any room between the traffic and parked cars.

I quickly shot past them and decided to get back on the street again. My brain said it would be cool to jump off the curb instead of waiting for a driveway entrance to rejoin traffic. This plan worked well—except for one small problem. When I jumped off the curb the chain fell off my bike. On a beach cruiser with a single speed, the chain is necessary as it also runs the coaster brake—an important function when going downhill.

I was gaining speed at an alarming rate with no apparent way to slow down, I tried putting my feet down to act as brakes but my flip flops quickly caught fire and I aborted that plan. I had to do something fast because at the bottom of the hill was a stop light and a tee intersection and I didn't think I could make the turn at my rate of speed. I began looking around for something to crash into. I spotted a perfectly manicured hedge up ahead and thought maybe that would be a good place for the paramedics to pick me up. I'm not sure how fast I was going when I hit the hedge, but it was fast enough to completely uproot two bushes and destroy another.

Once the dust settled I started assessing the damage. I immediately checked out my Hawaiian shirt to make sure it wasn't torn—it wasn't. I noticed that Pete had abandoned me and the hurdling death machine. I found him later in the bushes with no feet, he doesn't squeak the same now, I think he hates me.

I put the uprooted bushes back in place, picked up my chain and the remains of Pete—he'll eventually learn that pain lasts but a moment, but glory forever.

So if you are even feeling a little bored, grab a "funny-looking" old beach cruiser, a "funny sounding" squeaky parrot named Pete, and a brother-in law named Joe. Your parrot may unfriend you—but you might make new friends with the paramedics that come to pick you up. And boredom will never be in your vocabulary again—fear, trepidation, and pain perhaps—but never boredom.

Pink Pants, Invisible Clothes, and the Truth

"Sitting in the pool on the sundeck, overlooking the rolling waves, sipping a cold drink—does life get better?" I asked my sister as I lazily kicked my feet through the clear water. She was spritzing tanning lotion on her already brown legs. She stopped and set the bottle down.

"Really?" she asked. I could hear the eye-roll in her voice as she lifted one eye-brow at me.

"Well?" I questioned. "What part about that statement is wrong?"

"What part about that statement is right?" she shot back.

I pushed a floating toy car away from me as I leaned back in my kids' plastic wading pool, sitting atop our boathouse on the Columbia river.

"It's all true." I argued. "I'm in a pool, overlooking the water, a cold drink in my hand."

Once more she gave me a disgusted look, like only a sister can, "A half-drank glass of your kid's root beer slushy?"

"It's all in how you spin it," I laughed.

She shook her head, "You're crazy."

She went back to her book, and I went back to my slobbered on slushy while soaking in the little plastic pool. It's all in how you spin it.

Maybe that's what's going on with the news today. Every place you turn you hear "fake news," "fake news!"

It's all in how you spin it. As a kid there was a song I remember listening to about a man who was dating a woman he thought was really rich. She was always telling her boyfriend how her "daddy really cleaned up in Tennessee." The boyfriend was afraid of meeting her really rich father. When the time came, he was stunned to learn that her father was really a garbage truck driver—he really did clean up! The song ends when he says next time a girl says her daddy's big in Tennessee, he's just going to assume she means fat!

As a culture we claim we value honesty...but I am not so sure. Children are honest—and we try to change that from the time they can talk. Don't believe me?

A child walks up to their great-great-aunt, pushes on her polyester clad middle and says "You have a really big belly." The child's mother blushes deep red, scoops the child up, apologizes to her great-aunt and starts scolding the child. Another time, the child sits on grandma's lap and says "you have hair on your chin." Again, the mom apologizes, and scolds the child. The child wasn't incorrect—but he learns he can't speak the truth. We curb the truth out of politeness.

As the child grows, they become less honest. First out of politeness, then out of political correctness, and now, in today's society because truth seems ugly and offensive.

I'm reminded of the old fairy tale of the Emperor's new clothes. A couple of hustlers conned the Emperor into paying them to make the finest (and of course most expensive) threads that gold could buy. And the best part? Only wise people fit for their posts would be able to see it. The swindlers pocketed the beautifully expensive wares, while they sat at empty looms, daring anyone to examine the beautiful designs they were weaving into the cloth.

No person wanted to be thought a fool or unfit for their posts, so everyone admired the invisible cloth. The day of the procession came and the swindlers dressed the emperor in his invisible clothes. His noblemen made a big show of lifting the train as they carried it down the streets.

Only a small child had the honesty to say "But he hasn't got anything on." To which his father shushed him for his prattle. The Emperor shivered, and suspected he was right, but he straightened taller than ever and walked proudly as his noblemen held high the train that wasn't there. Those swindling weavers sure knew how to spin it!

Today, right is left, up is down, night is day, and purple is green. We're shushing the children that are speaking up, because the truth of sitting in 3 inches of water and drinking a slobbery slushy, isn't quite as beautiful as sitting in the pool, overlooking the rolling waves, sipping a cold drink.

We value beauty more than honesty. Just squeeze in to a pair of too-tight jeans and ask your husband how they look. I once watched a guy tell a girl she looked great in a hideous pair of hot pink leather pants—she didn't want honesty, he said, she just wanted to be told she looked great. Welcome to the pool!

The 8th Day of the Week

Have you ever reached the end of your week, barely making it halfway on your "To-Do" list? Starting out the week, on last week's list, seems a bit like combining with a hopper that never fully empties.

To keep the hopper emptied and the "To-Do" list short, one seems to have to ignite the midnight petroleum frequently, and then suddenly you find that "spontaneous napping" has somehow found its way to the top of your list. I finally got my 8 hours of sleep in—took 4 days—but who's counting?

Summertime seems to be the worst for uncompleted lists: always trying to squeeze an extra hour or two out of each day. Each morning we juggle the harvest balls of hay, wheat, and watermelons between us and the crew. If we are lucky we keep those balls bouncing between us long enough to eat breakfast—before noon!

Recently, sitting in the freshly cut hay, drinking a warm Gatorade, looking into a swather header that obviously felt it had put in its 8 hours and wanted to go home, I had an epiphany. Our lists aren't too long—our weeks are too short. We need an 8-day week. And I have the perfect name for it—Someday. Just think what we could get done!

How many times have you asked your spouse about building that extra room on your house? Or having a yard-sale to clear out the clutter? Or maybe building that treehouse for the kids? Ya, you'll get to that "Someday."

How wonderful would that be to have Someday roll around every week? I could finally get my sewing room completed. My husband could finally fix his old Trans Am that has held down the same piece of ground for close to 6 years now—okay, so that one might take 'a month of Somedays.' But just think of the things you've been needing to finish that would suddenly happen? I might actually get my Christmas tree taken down—but then again, if I just wait a few more months I'll be ahead of the game. Someday, I'll be on top of my housework. Someday, I'll learn that foreign language. Someday...

My husband interrupted my thoughts, "I got the header fixed, when do you want to finish swathing?"

"Someday," I smirked at him.

They say everyday is a gift, well, if that's true, then I'd like a receipt for Monday. I'd like to exchange it for "Someday."

The Flat Out Truth

I don't have all my ducks in a row. I don't even have them all in the same pond. I'm not even sure they are all ducks—there may be some flying squirrels in there. But I thought I had the basics figured out: the sun rises in the east, farming almost pays the bills, and gravity holds us onto this spinning ball we call Earth. That is until last week.

"Do you believe the earth is a globe?" was the start of the conversation.

"Um...yes...why?" I answered. Curious as to what kind of joke was about to be played on me.

"Just wondering," the lady replied. "It's possible it's flat."

I nearly choked on my orange juice. "Oh yes, flat...I thought we disproved that back in 1492?"

I was then presented with a list of 200 "proofs" that Earth is not the spinning globe most people believe it to be. It's actually the biggest conspiracy ever to be pulled off.

Sometimes the best thing you can do is just sit back, keep your mouth shut, and just let the crazy unfold.

"If the earth is round," she continued, "why are horizons

always flat?" I was then presented with a number of anomalies. Have you ever wondered why planes don't fly over Antarctica? It would be a direct route to many places...if the world was round. But it isn't. There is no such thing as the South Pole. And so the conspiracy begins...

Now, back to the curvature of the horizon. It is perfectly flat—therefore the earth must be flat. Don't bother responding about the large surface area of the earth or the International Space Station sending back photographs of the earth; you should be able to see the curvature if it existed and any photographs sent by NASA have been faked. They know this to be true because the clouds have words in them and there is a cartoon dog visible in the NASA photos of Pluto.

This is a conspiracy theory that swallows other conspiracy theories whole. Gravity is a hoax, space travel is a hoax. The sun and moon aren't what we have been told either. Some even believe the moon is just a projected hologram.

You may think the obvious question here is what would be the motivation behind a hoax on such a global...er I mean world scale?

"It just makes more sense," she kept answering. "Makes more sense as to why airplanes can fly without having to account for the curvature... Makes more sense for the moon to be a translucent disk having it's own light... Makes more sense as to why we can see things 140 miles away without them going off the horizon backward."

I just kept thinking Galileo would be turning over (I mean orbiting) in his grave about now. I had never thought, in my life, I would be defending my position on a moving solar system, or that the earth was spherical. I kept waiting for someone to pop out "You're on Candid Camera!" But no one popped up.

Later that day, I had to turn to the internet...and discovered that there is a whole society of people out there that believe the earth is flat. The more I read, the more surprised

I was to learn that the flat earth community has supporters all around the globe...okay, so maybe that pun fell flat! (haha)

After reading a few of their websites, I was even more shocked. These people posit that we are living on a cluster of continents, the oceans surround us and a rock or ice wall (protected by NASA) keeps us from falling off. Any arguments using physics or science will be met with "If you believe that hoax."

People have the right to their opinion to be sure. It's not like I have viewed Earth from space with my own eyes. But if the world isn't round and it doesn't spin, we wouldn't be able to take another trip around the sun. Moon pops wouldn't taste the same, and Star Trek would be total fiction. Oh, what an unbearable thought! I think I'll just put an out-of-order sticker on my head and call it a day—not to be confused with a revolution of the sun.

On the plus side, there would be no need to worry about Global warming! Maybe the man in the moon could toss down some of his green cheese, because after a day like this I may need something to go along with the wine!

What's in Your Lunchbox?

As the years have passed, the science of what food is healthy spans the spectrum. Red meat, white meat, fake meat, no meat, and then back to red. Mark Twain once wrote, "Don't take advice from a health book. You could die from a misprint!"

•Drink a glass of red wine a day. Studies show it helps build better bones, prevents blood sugar problems, boosts your body's defenses, can increase your memory power, and may increase life expectancy.

•Alcohol consumption can kill you. Studies show it raises overall death rates, causes cirrhosis of the liver, causes cancer, migraines and increases the risk of heart disease.

•Coconut oil has many health benefits. Studies show it is a natural prevention for Alzheimers, it prevents high blood pressure and heart diseases, it cures UTI's and kidney infections and also shows promise in preventing cancer.

•Coconut oil can harm your health. Studies show it will raise your bad cholesterol as much or more than animal fats, it will increase your chances of heart disease, and will lower your overall health.

I like science as much as the next guy. But historically it hasn't been very consistent when it comes to diet recommendations. Every year the theories change: wine saves you. Wine kills you. Coconut oil is the new miracle drug. Coconut oil is the worst saturated fat you can ingest.

Hippocrates, the father of western medicine, promoted wine as part of a healthy diet as well as preventing diarrhea. Then Prohibition outlawed any beverage with an alcoholic content of over 1.28% citing morals as well as health.

In the '80s, the *New York Times* said wine was linked to migraines, as well as causing acid-reflux. In the 90s, 60 Minutes said that red wine drinkers had lower cholesterol that their counterparts. Later it was said to stop macular degeneration, and prevent prostate cancer. Then in the early 2000s studies showed it may increase the likelihood of getting breast cancer.

Fourth of July. A time of celebration, a time to be thankful for our freedom, a time for friends, family, barbecues... and the ever-worsening discussions on food. "We only eat organic." "We don't eat any artificial colors or dyes." "We stopped eating dairy after we watched a documentary..." "No gluten for us." Barbecuing has now become an art....not just the actual cooking, but on how to keep peace between the carnivores and the vegans.

Inevitably someone will start in on the latest studies showing a particular food that is now a super-food (or super-villian, depending on the year) my husband will laugh and say, "I don't know, my mom ate it (or didn't eat it), and she died from cancer—course it could have been because she drank water too!"

This usually provides enough levity to change the conversation.

It's funny though, how animated people can get over food. Especially when science over the years can't even agree with itself. Is wine good for you or bad? Is coconut oil helpful or harmful? If you don't like the results of the studies this year...just wait...it's like the weather in Pacific Northwest... it'll change tomorrow.

Basically I'd say this leaves us free to forget the "food-science" as no one really seems to know or agree on what causes or prevents aging and cancer.

I would suggest eating and drinking what makes you happy, after all, studies show that happy people live longer...oh wait...new studies say pessimists. Oh mercy!

Studies on preservatives, carbs, calories, organics...it's just too much for me. I just hope I don't get the soggy cheetos that my baby stuck back in the chip bag after sucking off the cheese!

When I Said "I Do," I Meant "I Don't"

*H*ot water gurgled up around me as I sunk into the mineral water carved basins on the side of a cliff overlooking the cold rapids of the river below. The scenery was glorious. Rock basins filled with various temperatures of water cascaded waterfall-style down the side. It was a lovely way to spend an anniversary.

13 years ago we said "I do." And while I thought we were both on the same page as to what that meant...we weren't. It has taken many hours of tractor driving with all that alone time for me to finally put my finger on what went wrong...but it finally came to me. When we both said "I do," what we meant was "I don't."

"I don't" see the need to kill spiders any more. If I would have wanted to kill my own spiders for the rest of my life, I wouldn't have married a Spider Killer! So stop complaining, it doesn't matter that the spider is closer to me than you—it just means you must hurry faster before it reaches me! I'm pretty sure that was in the fine print of the marriage vows, "I don't have to kill spiders ever again as long as you are within screaming distance."

When I said "I do," I also meant "I don't" need to put fuel in my car...or DEF fluid, or change the oil, or install new brake pads... Yes, I know I am perfectly capable. Yes, I know I did those things (except the DEF) for nearly 10 years before we got married...but...you know what they say...women let it all go once they finally get married...and I let all that knowledge go. So if I run out of fuel, and have to wait alongside the road for assistance, expect that I will feel it is your fault.

"I don't" have to warm my own feet up anymore. I see no reason to bring a heating pad, or warm rice sock, or hot water bottle to bed in the winter anymore. I married my foot warmer. Since your legs and feet are always warmer than mine, it seems only fair to me that you allow me to press my feet-shaped ice cubes on your nice hot calves—I share my ice, you melt it.

When those vows were spoken there must have also been some unspoken clause that said shaving is no longer a priority for him. Before the vows, shaving occurred nearly every time we saw each other. After the vows were exchanged however, it became weekly for church...then, only for special church functions, then it was for the holidays, and now? I'm not even sure he knows where his razor is? The silver lining though (besides what's on his face) is that I have almost forgotten how to clean whiskers out of the bathroom sink!

"I do" for him, also meant "I don't" have to scan things into the computer ever again. Every time the computer acts up, one can almost read his thought-subtitles above his head: I don't have to worry about what programs I need to open documents, or how to save or attach files. I married my secretary. She can have the headache of not having the right kinds of file extensions, she can hook up all the electronic devices, cords, cables, tv, dvd, blue tooth set up, wi-fi...I don't want to know, I don't need to know, and besides I just used the instruction manual to kill her spider!

When he said "I do," he meant "I don't" need to pick up my dirty laundry anymore. I don't need to pick it up, nor do I need to wash it...or dry it, or fold it....because those sticky socks kicked off in the corner, magically become bleached and mated and tucked back into my drawers. If I wanted to do laundry or keep house I would have stayed single or hired a maid....instead I said "I do."

When someone tells us how long they have been married, my husband is usually quick to ask "But how many good ones?" So while we each went into "I do," thinking a little bit like "thank goodness I don't have to...." we have still enjoyed all 13 years of marriage.

I have run out of fuel a bit more than I was expecting, and he has run out of clean socks a bit more than he was expecting...but at the end of the day, I still get to put my cold feet on him, and he doesn't have to mess with the queing up our favorite Netflix episode...and the rest is rust and stardust...

High Maintenance Farm Girls

$\mathcal{M}$y sister and I are pretty low maintenance—or so I'd always thought. We are more likely to finger-comb our hair than use a brush, our combined yearly total for makeup is less than $20, our shampoo fragrance doubles as perfume, and the only shopping we tend to enjoy is at the Yamaha dealership. Someone once asked me if I ever do my nails... of course I do...unless it's the rare occasion I've forgotten my pocketknife. When our tank tops get too air-conditioned (i.e. holey) they become pajamas tops, and we can both pack for trips in just minutes.

Recently, however, I read a list that would make us just a bit more maintenance than I would have ever dreamed. Below is the list and my explanations as to why they seem to apply to farm girls.

8 ways to tell if a woman is high maintenance
8. She criticizes the clothes you choose to wear to a social event

I am so very guilty of this one. Many times as we're walking out of the house to go to a wedding, funeral, or family function, I glance over to see my husband wearing a shirt with grease stains, dirty jeans, and his work boots....that's when the criticizing begins...

7. She squints in disgust when you pull your vehicle up for her to get in.
Many times my nose has wrinkled as I move empty pop bottles, chip bags, old mail, and an assortment of other things that have far exceeded their shelf-life. Ugh...disgusting.

6. An overnight trip requires at least 2 pieces of luggage.
This is not due to 8 pairs of shoes, 4 bottles of moisturizer and lipstick to match every outfit. Instead, one usually has all of the clothes, toiletries, and books. and the other has rubber boots, leather gloves, coveralls, and a work coat...all the dirty things.

5. She takes her fluffy dog every where she goes. My dog has ridden with me, since she was 8 weeks old. She has ridden in every piece of machinery we own (the swather is her favorite), she also likes riding in the boat and can hang on amazingly well on the back of my four-wheeler at the sand dunes. She knows which fast-food restaurants give out treats, and has learned to hang her head just enough to get an extra treat at the bank.

4. She likes fur clothes
Refer to number 5. My dog is a long haired half-Pyrenees. I have fur lined clothes, furniture and vehicle upholstery.

3. She has a lot of guy friends
Um....maybe because girls are too much drama? And besides it's always more fun to be under the hood of a car than under the lights of a tanning bed

2. She prefers her water special...and turns her nose up at filtered.

Well really...who doesn't? I love the Columbia River and spend as much time there as our farming schedule allows... but given the choice between a tropical white sand beach, or a beach on the Columbia...well...I prefer special water too. And filtered water is so soft, scrubbing the day's grime off is a challenge.

1. She takes several hours to get ready to go to the store.

Guilty again. Just last week my husband begged me to go grocery shopping. Opening the fridge for breakfast he found mayo, ketchup, mustard, salad dressing, snow cone syrups, Worcestershire sauce, and a jar of maraschino cherries....not exactly the breakfast of champions. The cupboards held an onion and a bag of cat treats. It was easy to see shopping had to go on my list. But first I needed to flag the combine to the next field, give one of the guys a ride back to his pickup, and make a quick parts run. By then the wheat was dry, and I found myself in the combine. The moon was high in the sky before I was heading to town on a grocery run...15 hours later.

I think my sister and I must be pretty high maintenance after all.

Running...Behind

*C*hanging handline is good for strength training...but seems to fall short on the cardio. My husband seems to think if I want cardio than I should just run in between sets, or run carrying the pipe—making it twice the workout. Not one to expend energy needlessly, he was quick to take up Neil Armstrong's quote, "I believe every human being has a finite number of heartbeats, and I don't intend to waste one of mine running around doing exercises."

I have always enjoyed a good set of pushups, though I've never been real good on regular exercise. But that Caribbean cruise left me with more than just happy memories and beautiful photos. I decided to take up running...it was cheap and fit into my schedule. I've never run before...and with good reason. My mascara runs faster than I do!

Both of my sisters run, but I never did. My mom always told us not to run when we were kids. It wasn't until later that I realized she actually said we shouldn't run with scissors. Funny what a difference two words can make.

But with swimsuit season right around the corner, I had to

do more than a few pullups and pushups...it was time to put the scissors down and get a running buddy. I found one, and nearly every night we hauled our unwanted weight a couple of miles, hoping that we can outrun it. So far, I've had little to no success, however thankfully I have been able to outrun all the neighborhood dogs!

Each night, as we're sweating like pigs, my running buddy tells me how foxy we're going to look if we keep this up....she may be right...but for one thing. She's running towards this wonderful goal of a beautiful bikini body...and I'm running toward the delicious supper I know my husband will have ready when I get home.

I thought maybe I wouldn't be so ravenous if I ran in the morning instead. So I tried morning running...twice. But I discovered morning jogging isn't healthy. If morning joggers knew how tempting they looked to morning motorists, they'd stay home and do sit-ups.

I don't know if I'll ever outrun these unwanted pounds, but I guess at least I'm proving my doctor right. She said running would add years to my life...she was right. I'm sure I feel at least 5 years older already!

Maybe I should stick to handline...at least I've never been chased by a dog while changing pipe.

Persimmons and Cat Hair

Persimmons. A small reddish-orange fruit that I was completely unfamiliar with before meeting my husband 16 years ago. And in those 16 years that I have discovered them, I must say, I feel no great loss for the first 20 years of my life that I was blissfully unaware of them. But each fall we market and sell them, and my husband's family relishes the tart, astringent fruit, so sometimes I feel alone in my distaste of them. That is until this year.

While offloading some of the boxes of fruit, one of the neighbors stopped in to say hi. Having never heard of, or seen a persimmon before, my husband sent her home with a few to try. I must say I was curious as to what she thought. Would she be a believer, like so many, or would I finally have an advocate on my side for how strange they taste.

A few days later the curiosity got the better of me, and I emailed her asking if she'd tried them yet, and what she'd thought. Shy sent back a polite message saying "Well, I don't know, the persimmons made my mouth feel weird."

I typed back "Ya, they make my mouth feel weird too... kind of like gross!"

Her response back was quick and had tears running freely down my face. She had nailed my first, last and only experience tasting them to a T. I could almost hear her beautiful South African accent rolling the following words off her tongue:

"I don't know, it was almost furry, sort of hard to explain. My bottom teeth felt like someone had lined them with cat's hair or something. How do people eat those things? I was wondering if I did something wrong the way I ate it.

It was juicy and sweet, but oh heck, the aftermath was terrible! Never been so happy to use mouth wash and then that didn't even take the sensation away. Felt like my teeth were on edge sort of like when you accidentally tap your teeth on the metal part of a travel mug."

No longer am I alone in choosing mouthwash over persimmons. And the next day, my laughter was to continue. I received yet another message from my persimmon-loathing-friend.

"Oh boy! had to share this special info with you. Bargain Betty here, found an awesome sale for you...wait for it...I know the suspense is killing you and will probably put you in labor (let's hope not)...but here goes.

89 cents a piece for all the persimmons you can fit into your shopping cart at the local market! I told you, I found the deal of a lifetime..LOL! I am proud to announce I did not come home with any of those awful-tasting, hairy-ball-looking fruit thingies! Ugh! Give me a piece of unhealthy, smooth-melting chocolate any day!"

They say friendship is made of loving or hating a common thing. Well bring on the friendship; and for those of you that love persimmons? Wonderful, keep eating them! It leaves less to go to waste here.

And for all of you who haven't yet eaten one. I encourage you to try it. One never knows, you may have found your new favorite fruit! And if it happens to leave fur on the bottom of your teeth, and mouthwash doesn't seem to help, stop on by. The neighbor and I will be happy to let you indulge in left-over Halloween candy with us.

Baby Puke and Salesmen

My fingers were tingling with numbness as I bounced my baby on an exercise ball. It was one of those long, lousy days where baby was tired and crabby...which in turn made me tired and crabby.

The more I bounced the sleepier he got. The sleepier he got the louder his "you can't make me go to sleep" cries were. The louder they got, they shorter they became though. Soon his head started to loll against my arm which caused a welcome but increased tingling sensation as his body started to become dead-weight. This little boy is a chunk...we've laughed that buying clothes for him is like purchasing a computer. It's obsolete and outgrown before you've arrived home.

His eyes closed, my fingers numb on my right hand, and his whimpering barely audible now. A few more minutes of gentle bouncing and I would finally be able to get some much needed chores done. Like take a shower and get dressed!

I finally decided to chance it. I stood up. So far so good.

I kept up the bouncing-like motion in my arms as I headed for the bed. The thought crossed my mind that maybe I could just lay down too...only for a minute...how good it would feel to close my eyes and just—

That's when the doorbell rang. And not some sprightly 'ding-dong' ring. No, my 7-year old loves changing out the sound. A long dark organ dirge banged loudly through the speakers. Immediately a nap was out of the question...the baby let out a loud and angry scream, drowned out only by the still playing doorbell. Did I mention it was long?

With the doorbell still playing it's ghastly song, and the baby screaming at the top of his lungs, I opened the door—to a salesman. A door-to-door salesman. I felt like crying too.

The man tried really hard to ignore the screaming baby, the pajamas, and a hair do that looked like I'd slept in it for a week—I'm sure it couldn't have been more than a couple of days. He started his spiel and I kept trying to quiet a baby. Suddenly the baby spit up. Epically spit-up. Warm baby puke oozed down my shoulder and puddled in my elbow before making rhythmic splats on the deck.

The man looked down at his product and back up to a crying baby and a mom that was standing there in pajamas and baby puke and I think he realized his speech was going to be wasted.

He stopped mid-sentence, "Ma-am, I can see you're busy, you just have a good day, ya hear?" He nodded at me as he backed down the porch, away from the baby puke that was still glopping down my arm.

Later that day, I had fed the baby, and finally, finally gotten him to a light slumber—that's when the horrible doorbell rang again. The baby rolled and began fretting. I was torn between answering the door or trying to keep the baby asleep. I opted for the baby. I cooed to him, and rubbed his back.

The doorbell droned on for its one-minute song, and I released my breath when it ended. The baby was still sleeping. Then it rang again. No way could I keep him asleep for another minute of that racket. He was soon awake—thankfully not screaming. I scooped him up and headed for the door. Maybe it was important...after all they rang twice.

I guess it was important. It was a couple ladies inquiring about my eternal salvation and wanting to leave me pamphlets to read. As they started into their rehearsed questions, the baby leaned away from me and puked. Missing the one lady's shoe by less than an inch.

She looked up quickly, "I didn't realize your baby was sick," she stammered, thrusting the pamphlets into her purse and scurrying down the porch. Baby puke is like kryptonite to unsolicited visitors.

I headed back in the house, turned the ringer off the doorbell, and started thinking up a sign for the front door. I think it should be something like: "No Soliciting. We are too broke to buy anything. We know who we are voting for. We have already found Jesus. Seriously, unless you are giving away tractors, ammo, or have a package from Amazon...Go Away! We have Baby Puke, and we know how to use it!"

Lucy's Laundry Scheme

*D*ecember 5: Clean house, no visible laundry, fully stocked refrigerator, and freshly-shampooed hair.

December 6: Enter baby Parker

Fast forward two months: I'm sure there must be a clean corner of the house somewhere...maybe in the closet under the stairs? And laundry? Each day we're surprised by how a baby so small can generate enough puke to dirty shirts, pants, and socks, and that's without counting his own clothes he spits up on! No one even knows what's in the fridge...we've been living on take out and pizza. And no one can remember that squeaky clean soap smell...baby puke has taken over. And we're loving every dirty-soiled-hungry-smelly-minute of it.

Then a phone call announces company—lots of it. Three families over the course of the weekend. We look at each other with our tired, sleep deprived eyes, and go into panic mode.

The house itself was easy to throw together...but the laundry? There was no possible way to get it all washed before they arrived.

Nearly two months of laundry covered just about every surface in the house. Standing there looking between the dirty laundry and the clock, I had a Lucille Ball moment... we should just gather it all up and hide it in our bedroom. The plan seemed to work.

We entertained one couple Saturday afternoon, another couple Saturday night...and all was good. The laundry was hidden away, and we took great pains to keep both our bedroom door shut as well as the fridge door.

Then Ricky Ricardo showed up...in the form of a cousin from Utah, and blew my idea apart as quickly as Ricky usually shattered Lucy's. My cousin breezed through my carefully closed bedroom door and was suddenly knee-deep in my "dirty" little secret.

"Well," she stated cheerfully, "it looks as if we're going to have a girls night out...at the laundromat." I tried to argue. I told her I'd get around to it soon. I told her I'd rather visit with her. I came up with every reason/excuse I could think of to get her not to air out my dirty laundry. But it was no use. Soon we were at the laundromat sorting out life's problems one load at a time.

By the time we started folding the 14th dryer load, I was contemplating becoming a nudist...then I happened to catch a glimpse of my post-Parker body in the ceiling security mirror... I realized just what that would look like...and I kept folding.

Sitting there watching the washers and dryers spin and tumble, I remembered just how bad Lucy's ideas usually turned out...what a dumb person for me to emulate. And that's when I got my next Lucy idea. Laying on the laundromat folding table was an interior decorating magazine. It talked about using a pop of colorful cloth to jazz up a room. I glanced up at my load of reds swishing in suds, and then cheerful yellows tumbling brightly. Most people move throw pillows to sit down...how could decorative laundry be much different? I think I'll try adding a pop of color to all my rooms with carefully thrown laundry!

Hours later, our dressers were once again full, and it felt good to have it done. And I was grudgingly grateful to my cousin for making it happen—but as she went to grab a cold drink from the fridge to celebrate our hard work, I practically knocked her over to ensure I got there before she could open that door too!

The Farmer

Watermelon farmers never die...
they just go punky.

'Beautiful' Holiday Moments

My Holidays are like an Indiana Jones movie: adrenaline, possible treasure, strategy games, stress, and of course catchy music. Sometimes that means you find yourself with the holy grail, and other times you're hanging out in the snake pit—but it's always an adventure. This season was no exception.

"I hope you like your present this year," my husband said. I glanced at the calendar on the wall behind him. Less than one week til Christmas.

"I just hope I can come up with a present for you," I muttered under my breath. He and my dad are two of the most difficult people to get presents for. If they want it, they buy it. If they don't buy it, it's because it's out of their price range—which of course means out of mine.

"What was that?" he asked.

"I am sure I will love any present from you!" I smiled brightly. He looked suspicious, but didn't press me.

If agriculture is your occupation, you can be sure that money isn't always exceedingly plentiful. One just always hopes the good years outweigh the bad. Some holidays finances feel stretched tight as guitar strings—but in those years the gifts seem to be the most beautiful.

For it is when those strings are tight that the guitar can make beautiful music. The tighter the year, the more homemade gifts, which to me are always the most beautiful. Whether it's beautifully silly like a metal garbage can filled with kindling as a DIY keep warm kit (thank you dear brother-in-law), or just plain beautiful like an intricate wooden jewelry box handcrafted by my dad.

I think a two-way spousal radio would be a pretty beautiful gift too. It would transmit directly from one spouse's brain to the other. Think of the possibilities. Forget helmet coms. This would work silently with a limitless range. Sitting at a holiday meal, you could stop your spouse from telling a story that may be best forgotten.

When snowmobiling you could remind your more adventurous spouse that you will be very grumpy if he chooses that ridiculous side-hilling trail.

I bet many couples could benefit from this brain radio. It would make working animals so much easier—you could holler and scream and tell your spouse where to go—(I mean what animal to head off) without ever opening your mouth! My parents could really use this!

Of course, with this device, I wouldn't have been able to make a shirt that read "I will always love you... but I don't have to like you when we're working cattle." It was a beautiful Christmas gift...although I best not say which parent I gave it to!

A social filter would be a beautiful gift too. It would work by scanning the crowd, gauging the situation, and only allowing the most appropriate of stories, jokes and ideas to be audible—the rest would just get whisked away into the great abyss. It would make "No Filter Friday" a lot more meaningful.

But since those gifts will never work in reality... maybe I will just let him borrow my imaginary friend for a day. Which, as it turns out, wouldn't have been the worst gift he could have gotten—seeing as how my mom gave him a "pass the gas" game! Perhaps I need to design social filters for the whole family!

Thankfully that wasn't the only game that was given. We scrounged for batteries to install in many games this year. Why is it, that the three phrases that sum up Christmas seem to be, peace on earth, goodwill toward men, and batteries not included?

But it was worth the scrounging, as we played all manner of games. We played games where we were expected to cheat and lie—some of the family were especially good at these—again, it is probably best not to name names.

We balanced coins on our heads, made elephant sounds, rubbed our elbows on walls and wore toilet paper masks—yes there are pictures of all of these events. We also learned that my husband's spelling is atrocious. "I just keep waiting for my auto correct to kick in," he said after a particularly mutilated sentence he had written in yet another silly game.

We laughed and cried our way through yet another holiday season. Exuding hospitality to friends and family—which in case you didn't know, is making people feel at home...even when you wish they were home! Of course that would never apply to our friends and family!

But too soon (and yet not soon enough at times) it was all over, and we were welcoming in the new year—along with our new motto. (Play Indiana Jones theme music here, and imagine Harrison Ford's voice) "Whatever you do always give 100% —unless you are donating blood!"

Electronic Sentiment

There we were surrounded by boxes of our "have-to-have its." Items that seemed we couldn't live without at the time, but now, with a new addition to the family, seemed to be taking up too much space. We had agreed it was time to downsize to gain more room, and it seemed a task best accomplished together. We had designated one area for Goodwill, another for junk, and another for things we really couldn't live without. We stood back to back, ready to conquer our boxes of treasures and trinkets. We had decided to use the philosophy that if it wasn't useful or beautiful it had to go.

"Well, no better time than the present," my husband said, sliding a box over to me. I sighed, and opened the lid.

Photographs of my husband's ex-girlfriends fluttered onto the floor. "Well," I laughed, "we can certainly toss this box out!"

My husband glared at me, and held up some of my old college textbooks "And while we're at it, these musty books can go."

"Not my books! No one gets rids of books—books are

always useful!"

I "rescue" my books and he "saves" his exes, and we move on to the next set of boxes with just a little less enthusiasm.

"We can definitely get rid of all this dark room equipment," my husband says. "Look at all this junk—I think you have more than 10 boxes of chemicals and supplies, not to mention these huge enlargers. Moving that out will free up the entire storage room!"

"But I love developing my own pictures," I protest. "It's both useful and beautiful."

"When was the last time you used any of this stuff? You went digital."

"Ya, well..." I was thinking hard. "Maybe I could teach Keagan?" I suggested. "It'd be a great learning opportunity."

"Are you really trying to justify this junk with school?"

"School. Yes! An elective. It would be a great way to teach him about film and photography. I'm going to keep it. It's useful."

"Come on, " he looked at me incredulously. I set my chin determinedly—finally he shrugged."There are three enlargers. Can you at least pick just one?"

"Well," I said slowly, "maybe that one." I pointed to the smallest of the three.

"Great!" he exclaimed, picking up the other two and heading toward the empty Goodwill area.

"No No!!" I shouted. "I meant we can get rid of the little one—I want to keep the big ones."

My husband wrinkled up his nose and gave me a look. "You'll never use this stuff," he grumbled.

But his attention quickly shifted as I tossed a large chain full of keys into the discard box. He scrambled over to retrieve them. "What are you doing?" he asked. "Do you know what these keys go to?"

"No," I said, "what?"

"Well I don't know," he answered, "but you shouldn't just throw them away without finding out. We might need one of them."

"They've been in this box since we got married—12 years ago."

"Look," he said, "this one goes to my Trans-Am."

"You mean the Trans-Am you sold before we even met?" I asked.

He shot me a look, letting me know that keys to locks on vehicles more than a decade gone were more than just junk.

It went on this way for several hours. The area designated "have-to-have" was piled high with boxes, the junk box held a few holey socks and some old Christmas cards, and the Goodwill area had three backpacking books, the littlest of the photo enlargers, two empty key chains, and an egg cooker. The egg cooker was the only thing we were both happy to see go.

Packing the one, lone Goodwill box out of the house, we both agreed that with Christmas coming up, instead of more stuff, maybe we should just email or text pictures of things to each other...it would be electronic sentiment without the clutter.

Farm Commodities & Indecisive Squirrels

"I think we should plant some timothy grass for next year," my husband said one morning. "I've been looking at the market prices and talking to some people, and I think that the North Field would be a good one for it." He then showed me some figures he'd jotted down, and all the reasons why it would be a good idea.

"Okay," I nodded in agreement, while trying to get the tea pot on the stove with a baby hanging off my leg and the cat screeching to be let out and the dog barking to come in.

"See these figures?" he asked, pushing more information across the table toward me. I glanced at them. "I think this would pencil out a lot better than the alfalfa that's planted there now."

I nodded, trying to unload the dishwasher while keeping the hanging baby on my leg away from the shiny dishes. Every once in a while I'd get too close and he'd 'help' by plucking a dish out of the drainer and dropping it on the floor.

"But then again," my husband was saying "we could

maybe grow corn in that field...." He started furiously scratching in his notebook.

"Momma, we need to eat breakfast so we can be filled up like squirrels," my son said. I had to smile, he's been learning metaphors and similes in school, and our life has become one bizarre simile after another.

The tea pot whistled. "The French toast will be done in a minute," I answered him "Do you want some tea while it's cooking?" He nodded and I poured 3 mugs of hot chai. I set one in front of my son and started sipping on another one.

"Are you going to drink both of those cups? Or are you going to share?" my husband bantered, finally taking a moment to look up from his crop planning.

"You know my caffeine intake is only recreational on Sunday...the rest of the week it's medicinal" I exclaim, grudgingly passing him the second mug of tea. He rolled his eyes at me, and took a big sip before delving back into his world of commodities and pricing.

"I think we could really make it work," he said.

"So let's plant some timothy," I agreed.

"No, not timothy. I think that Austrian peas would be really successful. It would allow..." his voice faded into the cacophony of our home as the cat was now yowling to come back in and the dog was barking to go out. "...more successful than barley..." he was saying. Sometimes I think successful is just getting the laundry out of the washing machine before mildew sets in.

"Yes, successful." I nodded.

I reached for my cup of tea...it was empty. How? When? I poured myself another mug. I don't drink that much, I told myself. I only consume tea on days that start with T. Tuesday, Thursday, Today, Tomorrow, Thaturday, Thunday. My reverie was broken with loud bagpipe music coming out of my son's room. "Momma, don't you think that is a sad song? Sad, like when you are out of cookies..."

"Well? What do you think?" my husband was asking.

"Uh, huh...Austrian peas...sounds good to me."

"Austrian peas?" my husband questioned. "I was talking about growing pumpkins."

"Pumpkins?"

"Yes, I was thinking that..." he went on showing me more scribbles in his notebook. The cat started yowling again at the door. Cats don't believe in the adage "when life shuts a door, a window opens." No. The cat's philosophy is "when life shuts a door...open it again. It's a door...that's how they work!"

"Or barley? What do you think of barley?" my husband asked again.

"I don't know, I don't care! Just pick something and plant it. Right or wrong. Make a decision and stick with it! The road of life is paved with flat squirrels who couldn't make a decision!"

My husband looked up surprised, then replied, "I'll remember that next time you're shoe shopping."

When is it Ripe?

"Hey, I've got a melon growing in my garden, how do I tell when it's ripe?" This seems to be the most common question I'm asked in the summer.

Followed by, "How can you pick out a good one?" I get asked that probably as often as my soon-to-be-30-year-old sister gets asked about marriage (Happy Birthday Sis!). At first, I arrogantly assumed I was asked this because my family has been growing Hermiston watermelons since 1934... but it's quickly apparent that I knew much less about melons than I'd once thought.

Sometimes people show me a photo of their prized garden melon; they only had one grow, so they don't want to pick it until it's ripened to perfection.

"Well it depends on the variety, the color..." And lately this is where I've been interrupted to tell me they know about the color. After all they read an article on the internet that describes a "prominent yellow spot." Without this spot it isn't ripe. And it needs webbing. This is a coarse brown material that is caused when the bees pollinate the flower and scar the membranes that later form fruit. "The more pollination = more webbing = sweeter fruit."

"Oh...." I smile and nod, "well it sounds like you've got it under control then." Usually this is when they turn to the bins of melons I have at the market and start asking where the yellow spot is. And why we don't have "more pollination" in our melons? Because after all, the internet says that's what makes them sweeter.

What can I say to that? "Who am I to disagree with a prominent internet entity," I laugh.

At this point they'll often start rolling over the melons looking for bright yellow spots. "Here, this is the webbing it was talking about it." they'll say, pointing at a melon with rough brown scars across it. "And you want to look for 'black hard globs seeping out' because that means it has so much sugar inside it's leaking."

When someone knows more about your livelihood than you do, it's often just best to step back, watch silently, and smile your inside smile.

After digging through most of the bin a cry of "Look, I found a sweet one!" marks the nearing end of this kind of melon encounter. A small, sunburned melon was held up jubilantly. It had heavy scarring on it, and a tiny bit of black sap sticking to it. It wasn't the one I would have picked to eat...but then again, I hadn't read the article yet on how to correctly pick a good one. My sister commented that it must have been dumb luck that has got our family through the last 80 years of melon farming. How did anyone grow or pick anything before the wisdom of the Internet?

I suddenly realize they are staring at me...waiting...for what? I can't remember. I look at them blankly.

"Our melon?" they question again. "How can we tell when it's ripe?"

"Well," I shrugged, "I guess I'd just cut it open...if it's red and tastes good it's ripe. If it's pink and tastes bland, it wasn't."

I watched the knowing look they shot between themselves which seemed to shout "See, we knew that article was the way to go!"

Last night, I received another, "When will my melon be ripe?" question. I rarely give people a definitive answer—melons being so subjective and all—but this time I felt my years growing up in a melon patch allowed me this answer. "Probably never...but I think you've got yourself a nice squash."

Weed it and Reap

There are two seasonal diversions that ease the bite of winter...spring thaw and seed catalogs. It's always exciting to flip through the pages and pick out your old-standbys: tomatoes and cucumbers as well as a few unusual and bizarre varieties like romenesco or samphire.

Everywhere you look you can see people getting ready for garden season: raised bed, fresh mulch, new tomato cages. Even the newspapers get into the season with garden tips: how often to water, and how to distinguish between weeds and plants.

Personally, I find the best way to differentiate is to give the plant a tug. If it came out easily, it must have been a good plant. If the roots have grown to China, and pulling on it only results in breaking the top off before toppling onto your backside—it's a weed.

"Grow Great Potatoes Easily" read the headline a magazine article promoting old, wet straw bales for home vegetable gardens. After loading several decomposing bales one evening, I started thinking about trying it myself. After asking my husband his thoughts, he reached over and took my hand "You have always been able to grow potatoes so well...I don't think you need straw bales to make them any better."

I gave him a proud smile. He took my hand, "let's take a little walk." Hand in hand we walked toward the garage. I was still smiling proudly when he reached for a box under a bench. It was full of last year's forgotten potatoes with 10-inch sprouts on them.

"If you can grow potatoes without dirt, why would you need straw?" The Bible was right—my pride went before destruction.

I don't necessarily love gardening, but I enjoy having the ability to run out and grab a fresh tomato or cucumber for supper. Having fresh produce and herbs on hand is great, but garden-maintenance is always a struggle. Mother Nature and I seem to have a bit of a misunderstanding in regard to my garden patch. I think of it as a place to raise food for my family to eat...she thinks of it as a CRP ground that is lacking in lambs quarter and kochia weed—and she tries hard to correct the error.

You can bury a lot of troubles digging in the dirt... perhaps that's why so many people finding gardening so relaxing. I've even seen cute signs that say "gardening is cheaper than therapy—and you get tomatoes!" But to me, gardening requires a lot of weeding and water...both that seem to come in the form of perspiration.

Anyone who wants to rule the world should try ruling a garden first. Once you can conquer squash bugs and slugs; successfully create country lines that are strict on the entry of terrorists like gophers, deer and rabbits; combat seasonal distresses such as flooding and drought; and still find yourself with enough energy, manpower and money to successfully harvest enough of your crop to generate an income—whether in the form of home canning or a lower grocery bill—then I think you can turn your attention to world power.

Some people really love their garden plants—even to the point of speaking to them. Pointing to para-science studies that show that plants thrive when spoken to. But either my plants never read those journals or my tone of voice is too harsh. When I'm in the garden, breaking the tops off weeds, I'm rarely in my "happy vocabulary." I think it really is because my plants are shy, and too much attention would inhibit their growth and cause them embarrassment—at least that's the theory I'm going with.

Some people get even more personal than just talk. I recently read that the month of May hosts a world naked gardening day. It claims to be an opportunity to pull weeds, plant flowers and harvest vegetables while getting some sun (where it doesn't usually shine). If you want to join them, feel free (literally), but my plants are wall-flowers...I am certain that kind of display would cause them to tuck in their blossoms and die of embarrassment. Regardless of your gardening style, the season is upon us.

My gardening motto has been, 'Early to bed and early to rise...work like a horse and fertilize!' Unfortunately, the only things that I can count on growing to maturity are puncture weeds and zucchini. Although I guess now I can add forgotten potatoes to that list.

Without Farmers...

A thin layer of intricate frost sticks to the green hood—slowly melting with each throaty puff of diesel as the tractor warms up. I love the smell of farming in autumn. It's my favorite season. Not because of pumpkin spice —but because harvest is finally slowing down. We actually have time to eat and brush our teeth in the morning...and by Christmas we'll probably even have time to sit down for meals as well!

Farming is sometimes romanticized...

Advertisements often show gorgeous girls in sundresses and boots in rolling wheat fields. Mother's babywearing children in expensive wraps walking through idyllic fields of frolicking lambs.

Farming is sometimes demonized....

I once saw a shirt that read: "farming: the art of losing money while working 400 hours a month to feed people who think you are trying to kill them." To which I would respond "don't gripe about a farmer with your mouth full."

But farming to me, is just a set of catastrophes that have resulted in a lifestyle. A lifestyle that I wouldn't trade for anything—although 8-hour days and paid vacations seem pretty tempting!

Everyone has probably seen the bumper sticker that says "Once in your lifetime you'll need a doctor, a lawyer, a policeman and a preacher. But you need a farmer three times a day." Agriculture is important and it goes beyond mere starvation.

Without farmers...there would be no farmer's tans.

Without farmers....who would be outstanding in their field?

Without farmers...there would be no corn (whiskey), rice (sake), sugarcane (rum), wheat (beer), grapes (wine), agave (tequila).

No farmers—no shot glasses.

Without farmers...there would be no tractors. And a feud as big as the Hatfields and McCoys would never have taken place: Red Tractors vs Green Tractors. Farmer born and farmer bred...this girl's tractor will never be red.

There are so many things that are impossible without farming.

Without farmers...

...there are no country roads to take you home...

...what happens in the barn...wouldn't...

...no one could be sheepish...or the black sheep...

...no one could have a cow anymore...

...life would be hard to live high on the hog...

...partying wouldn't be the same if the cows have no place to come home to...

...no one would chew the fat...

...you couldn't farm out your kids to their grandparents anymore...

...agriculture wouldn't be worth a hill of beans...

...there would be no first straw, so there could never be a last straw...

...you can't bet the farm...

...there would be no spring chickens...or old biddies...or need to worry about putting all your eggs in one basket...

...there would be no reason to make hay while the sun shines...

...no one would understand reaping or sowing...let alone reaping what you sow...

But the biggest travesty of all?

Without farmers...there would be no farmer's daughters...!

Private Detectives and Toenails

*W*aiting to get my trailer of watermelons unloaded, I sat inside the back of the grocery store and listened to a radio program about failing marriages and how to fix them. Several wives called in and admitted to hiring detectives to follow their husbands. The melons were unloaded before the program was over, but as I got in the pickup to continue on my deliveries, I couldn't help but think what the pictures would show if I was to hire a private detective to follow my husband. I think they would prove that he didn't really use the coupons that he said he had. And maybe catch him feeding some of the lunches I packed to the dogs, while he ate at Taco Bell.

Marriage really isn't that difficult, it's just a matter of coming to mutual understandings. He has to remember which hand towels are for every day use, and which are for (in the words of my husband) "the better people who visit my wife's home..." And I have to keep my mitts off his shop towels, (he says I use too many, and I never bring the roll back.)

This usually works well for us. The only time that understanding wears thin is when we're packing for trips. It doesn't matter if it's an overnight trip or a 2-week vacation, this seems to be the packing formula:

I pack my stuff, the kids' stuff, and make arrangements for the pet care. Meanwhile my husband has clipped his toenails.

I clean out the food in the fridge that might die in our absence, and straighten up the house, because if something happens—I don't want the neighbors to know we're slobs. And while I'm dumping the garbage, I see that my husband has found a chore entirely unrelated to our trip, and deeming it the utmost importance, insists it must be completed before departure: something like organizing the sockets in his toolbox, changing the filter in the heater, sorting through the pile of magazines in the end table, or calling some long-lost relative he hasn't talked to since last vacation that he suddenly needs to talk to now.

Then I will call the family to say goodbye and give them a rough itinerary (just in case), ask friends or neighbors to keep an eye on the house, and pack the pick-up with some last minute toys and books for the kids. And before I make my last trip out of the house, my husband is standing beside the vehicle asking why I'm not ready yet?

I remember spending weekends with my grandparents as a kid. My Grandma would be scurrying around getting all us grandkids ready for church, and my Grandpa would be sitting in the car honking the horn. When I was little, I found it funny—I must say, with age and understanding, it's a lot less funny than it used to be.

One of the marriage tips in the radio program I'd been listening to, said, "Before you assign blame, take a breath and ask your partner for his perspective."

That's when I learned I didn't know how he wanted the sockets, so that was a job he needed to do. I would have thrown away the wrong magazines—so that was also a job he needed to do. And he's never heard me volunteer to clip his toenails—although he'd be willing to let me—if I was that upset about it. And as far as me packing all the kids' stuff? Well I was doing such a great job, why interfere with perfection?

Take a breath, take a breath. I think I'm going to double my coupon clipping, just to give him a few more opportunities to feel guilty about throwing them away!

Car Fliers

A plastic key, a scratch card, a flier with matching numbers...are all things my husband loves getting in the mail. "You're a winner..." the car flier reads, and somehow all the rest of the small print goes unnoticed. He is certain that sooner or later he will win the grand prize. So far his winnings are much more, well modest is a nice way to put it.

We hadn't been married long when I first discovered this crazy habit of his. I had brought the mail in the house and was sorting it over the trash can, when he hollered. I had just thrown away a plastic key attached to a flier advertising a parking lot sale for a car dealership. One lucky winner would drive away in a new car. And "every" person that came in could win one of four prizes. It was junk in my eyes...and a treasure waiting to be claimed in my husband's.

He revived it out of the trash and headed up to bring home millions. Two hours later he returned with a chintzy block of 6 steak knives. One of which broke in half the first time I used it. He has also come home with a $5 Wal-mart gift card, a coupon book for stores we don't have in town, a compass that could no more tell north than a dutch oven and a pair of binoculars that didn't zoom. We have discussed how futile trying to win one of the real prizes is, but he is stubborn and determined that one day...if he goes often enough....

One day I penciled out how much this craziness of his was costing us. He had fuel invested in driving to the lot, and the time he spent listening to their sales pitch for a new car, and how his "treasures" just ended up in the trash can—which we were also paying for. It really wasn't cost or time effective. I am pretty sure though, that none of my sage advice was even heard, let alone heeded.

It wasn't long before another flier came in the mail. I try to toss them before he sees them, but this time I wasn't fast enough. He saw the grand prizes of cash and a new car, and I could see dollar signs roll around in his eyes. He snatched up the advertisement, and commented delightfully that the sale was going on now! I rolled my eyes, but I'm sure he didn't notice.

"If you're going to go up there," I said, "you could at least deliver my load of watermelons. It's close to the car sale."

He happily agreed, and told me he'd come home with cash. I made some kind of noise that could have been taken for agreement...but was probably more like a subtle snort.

Later that day I was stunned, when he came home with a fistful of cash and a big grin. His prize had been a cheap trinket, but instead of the salesman selling him a car, my husband had sold him watermelons! The harder the salesman pressed him to buy a vehicle, the harder my husband pressed to buy a bin of melons. As money was finally exchanging hands, the manager came out and remarked how the first sale of the day hadn't been theirs. "If you ever need a job..." he smiled, shaking my husband's hand.

At home, my husband gloated "I told you I'd come home with cash." I couldn't argue. He had, he did, and it looks like I still can't throw away the junk car fliers.

Little Jack Horner's Cantaloupes

*L*ittle Jack Horner must have been a cantaloupe eater. Who else intentionally sticks their thumb into food they intend to eat? Growing up in a family that raises melons for a living, gives one a unique perspective from which to people watch.

I have seen perfectly good cantaloupe be pressed and squeezed time and again by one potential buyer after another until the end becomes soft and mushy. Then people become eager to buy it because it has suddenly become "ripe."

Yes, a cantaloupe will get softer as it gets older....happens to the best of us....but I wouldn't call it "more ripe," unless you're talking about the smell. Which is the second thing people do after they have found a cantaloupe with a mushy end—smell it. A perfume bottle that has been broken will be more aromatic than one that is still sealed....perhaps that's why everyone wants to break the cantaloupe seal by pushing on the ends?

Cantaloupe get off pretty easy though, they only get poked and smelled, people picking out watermelons have a whole repertoire of methods to determine goodness. I have seen people water-witch melons with drinking straws, scratch the skin, look for curlycues and "bee stings", and so many more unusual things looking for a good one. So it was quite a surprise last week when I learned "the proper way" to pick one out.

I had delivered a load of melons to an establishment; the first bin had been taken off and set in a prominent location at the front of their store—giving me a perfect place to people watch while the rest of the melons were being unloaded. I didn't have to wait long.

A young man walked up and started looking over the bin of melons. He moved some around, and then without taking one, headed inside. Moments later, the proprietor comes out and begins giving him a lesson on choosing a good one. She picked up a melon and lifted it to her ear, then she started thumping on it. I was too far away to hear everything being said, but as he tried, she shook her head and told him he needed to press it tightly to his ear.

I wanted to ask if he was listening for the ocean? His conscience? A little voice that said, "pick me, pick me!!?" Instead I just watched as he hefted first one melon then the next to his shoulder, mashed it into his ear and pounded away on the outside.

Sometimes I wonder if people just make things up just to see other people look silly doing them? I wonder if I could start a new method where you give melons butterfly kisses and depending on how much dirt clogs your eyelashes that's when you know you've got a winner.

Makes me wonder about Little Jack Horner's mother who baked the Christmas pie. I'm sure if asked she would have had a much different (and cleaner) way to tell if the pie was good besides sticking your thumb in it.

There are a few times while picking cantaloupe you may "stick in a thumb, and pull out a plum," but no one ever says "oh that's a good one, let's eat it!" Instead, there are groans and fussing and the offending fruit is flung away. Soft is just a stepping stone to rotten—regardless of what Little Jack Horner thinks.

Dead Sheep & Candy Canes

I sat in stunned silence as the old 8mm video panned across a field of dead sheep, before stopping with a close up of a stiff ewe. I had heard the story years before, of how my Grandpa had bought a herd of sheep, just to have them die shortly after of liver flukes. Times were hard, and the wool was worth quite a bit of money, so everyone (kids included) went out and plucked the wool off the dead animals—farm families don't let assets go to waste, regardless of the smell.

Like family stories so often are, I had assumed that it had been exaggerated with the passing years. But here I was, watching the spinning, splotchedy film document their family outing. I was horrified. It was all true. Their girls, the youngest looking about 6, were all participating. I didn't know which was worse: that their little girls really were plucking away? Or that my grandmother had videoed it?

Then I started to laugh, a deep belly laugh. I hadn't thought I'd smile again, but the quirkiness that was so endearing in life, suddenly made her passing more bearable. My laughter didn't mean the damage cancer caused hasn't existed, just that the cancer was no longer in control.

"She...was quite a lady," one of the sympathy cards read. And it was right, she was. My grandma was a little bit parent, a little bit teacher, and a little bit best friend. All rolled into one huggable, loveable little lady with a hint of mischief always twinkling in her blue eyes. And through that unexpected mischievousness of filming the dead sheep, I found myself smiling once again.

It made me think back to the passing of my other grandmother. We were still shedding tears when it came time to open her safe. She had given the combination to two people—both were different, and neither worked. After a bit of debate, the guys decided to hack into it...literally. Out came the axes and torches, and after a few hours they had broken through.

Inside the safe, we discovered my grandmother's most valuable possessions—treasures so special she had locked them away and thrown away the combination. There were no important documents, no priceless jewelry, instead it was filled with—candy canes. Every flavor of candy canes imaginable. Candy canes so old one couldn't tell where the plastic ended and the candy started.

It was just what we needed to break out the smiles and the laughter. I thank God for dead sheep and candy canes. Those quirky memories provide a way to hold on to the things you love, the things you are, the things you never want to lose, without quite so much pain.

Melon Vision Goggles

*B*orn and raised on a watermelon farm means you get accustomed to a couple of things: a nice tan, well-developed biceps and the question "how can you tell if a melon is ripe."

When I was younger I used to try in earnest to answer the question. Explain about how different varieties have different tells, the coloring of the melon, and most importantly the sound. I remember watching their eyes glaze over about mid-way through my spiel. As I got older I condensed my answer picked them out a good melon, and still quite often their eyes would glaze.

Not long ago, my dad was asked the age-old question, and as he answered it, I suddenly realized what all my earlier answers had lacked...creativity.

My dad began by explaining about "the thump" and you you listen for the way the sound vibrates. But when he noticed the eye glaze, he changed tactics. No one wants the exercise regime...they want the diet pill.

"you could thump it...but everyone does that. When you want to know for sure, we use these special glasses..." The guy's eyes unglazed and he began to show real interest. My dad smiled, "melons have a little thing that pops up just like a turkey when it's ready. And with these glasses you can see it!" The guy quickly realized he'd been had....

I giggled about that all day...and all evening...and all the way across the road to meet the new neighbors. I'd taken a couple of small melons over as a welcome to the neighborhood, so it wasn't surprising that the inevitable question was asked: "how can you tell when a watermelon is ripe?" They had just picked one out of the garden that day and it had been green. I started in on color and sound...and I could see the girl's eyes beginning the glazing process. "...but for our pickers, we buy special glasses," I added. Immediately her interested piqued. "The glasses allow the pickers to see special designs in the melons that determine when they are ripe."

"Wow! That's amazing!" she exclaimed. "Where do you get them?"

"Oh, we special order them from China," I said, my lips beginning to twitch, "in bulk."

"Where could we get a pair?" she asked excitedly.

Unfortunately, I couldn't keep a straight face, or I may have made my first sale on our new line of Melon Vision Goggles.

They look like sunglasses, but when the humidity is at exactly 64.7% and you have adjusted your soil pH to 7.2, your watermelons will begin to shimmer with geometric designs. Each design can be decoded to determine if the melon is ripe, over ripe, or green. If you mail in two box tops, a gift certificate to my local hardware store, and only 2 easy installments of only $9.95, you too can be a proud owner of the one of a kind, Gullibility Goggles....er I mean, Melon Vision Goggles...void where prohibited or where gullibility isn't common.

A Combine, a Dresser and a Lawn Mower

It's good to try a little role reversal in your marriage every once in a while. If not just for the learning experience, but the revelations that always seems to come with it. For the last 10 years I have been the keeper of the laundry: sorting, washing, folding, putting it away, and tossing out holey socks.

Once after a particularly hectic period of farming, my husband noticed he didn't have many mated socks in his drawer. "Guess it's time to buy some more," he muttered as he crawled into bed. I looked at the big stack of his dirty socks in the basket of whites—wow, I wish I had magic drawers like he does. Continuously restocking his clean clothes, folded or mated, until the time he needed to buy more. Grunting in disgust I picked up the laundry basket and headed to the washing machine before crawling into bed beside my already snoring husband.

So recently, we decided to try a little role reversal. In the evenings, I climb into bed with a book and my husband trudges downstairs with the laundry baskets. After the first washed load he became frustrated as he tried putting them away. We share a chest of drawers.

"Where am I supposed to put this?" he grumbled.

I couldn't help but smirk, "Welcome to my world, why do you think I fold the laundry vertically? I can fit more in that way."

He grumbled and muttered and soon the laundry baskets became home to the clean laundry. After only 2 weeks, he came home grinning like a school boy. He had purchased a gorgeous dresser and chest of drawers.

"If I'm gonna do laundry, there's gotta be a place to put it!" The new bedroom furniture was beautiful, and while I loved it, I couldn't help but remember how he'd thought our one old dresser was satisfactory—until he had to use it. Hmmmmm....

Not too long after, I sat down at the computer and noticed a web page of riding mowers. Years ago, we had an old riding mower, one that needed TLC every time I started it. The tire had 4 plugs and a bottle of green goop, and still wouldn't hold air; the battery wouldn't hold a charge; the ignition didn't work; and you couldn't push the clutch and brake at the same time because of a linkage problem.

One day after 45 minutes of tinkering and a hand that was still smarting from the shock when I tried to spark across the battery with a screwdriver, I muttered "I'd get this lawn mowed faster with a push mower!"

Guess what arrived weeks later...for Mother's Day. Yep, my very own push mower. And if that wasn't enough, my husband hired my mowing services out to a neighbor widow to pay for my new Mother's Day present. And now I see, that after only one time of using my push mower, he's in the market for a riding mower?

I thought about the time I was driving combine with a sprained foot, it was in an air-cast and I was on crutches. The combine's air conditioner had broke and it was so hot the chickens would've laid boiled eggs. To keep the swelling down in my foot, I had a bucket of ice to put it in. The glassed cab of that combine was a sauna and I was constantly wiping the sweat (and chaff) out of my eyes.

"The season's almost done," my husband said one night as I was complaining, "I don't want to have to charge the AC, just for a few days before I park it for the winter."

The second to last day of wheat harvest, I played "Gopher" and headed out on a parts run, while he climbed into the combine. Imagine my surprise when coming back home a few hours later to see the combine parked in the yard...and the AC man working on it.

My eyes narrowed as I stared at the screen of the pretty new JD riding mowers. Then my lips started twitching... maybe I was looking at this all wrong. I knew this role reversal wouldn't last forever, and soon I was going to be putting the laundry away, and mowing my own yard...and besides the neighbors have an awfully big yard that needs mowed. If I play my cards right, I can get a riding mower and have my husband work it off.

Financial Advice from a Pug Dog

"*I* just saved $150,000 at the auction" my dad's text read, "just think what I can do with that extra money?" No, he didn't switch to Geico, or win the lottery, he just didn't win the piece of machinery he wasn't bidding on at an auction.

Yes, you read that right; let me explain this financial logic. As kids, my siblings and I learned about sheep and cows from our mom, poems and nursery rhymes from our grandmother, all about tattling from our cousins, discipline from our dad, and finances through an old movie: Life with Father.

I'm certain my parents had no idea to what extent that movie would become integrated into our lives when they brought home that VHS.

Never before would we have thought of stamping a foot and shouting "Ye Gads!!" at the top of our lungs. But while the movie may have added a little to our vocabulary, it was nothing like the influence it has had on our money handling skills. It turned us into savers.

A whole family of savers. And we don't just save pennies, we save hundreds of thousands of dollars which we've never seen, never had, and probably never will.

There is a classic scene in the movie where the son wants to buy a new suit, but the father says there is no need for such frivolity, he has an old suit his son can wear that will fit perfectly. The son is downcast, but what is there to do? Father has spoken.

Meanwhile the mother is out shopping and has bought a perfectly hideous statue of a pug dog for a surprising amount of money. When the father finds out he is most upset and shouts "Ye Gads!" while stomping around and explaining to her the value of money. He demands she return it. Which she did.

Soon a package comes to their house, and it turns out to be a new suit for their son. The father becomes angry and said he wasn't going to pay for a new suit. To which the mother blithely responds that she had actually got the suit for free because she had traded it for the pug dog.

He tries to explain that she had to pay for one or the other. She reminded him that she couldn't have paid for the pug dog, she no longer had it, and there was no money that exchanged hands for the suit. She had saved money.

You don't have to return pug dogs or clip coupons to save money, Try this simple money saving idea. Flip through the grocery fliers. Find something you don't like. See the honey-baked ham for $79.95. Being a vegetarian I won't eat it, so I won't buy it, and I have just now saved $79.95. Sounds easy, huh?

Now that you have mastered a small amount let's move on to something bigger. Go to your local hardware store and sit on the riding mowers. You find the one you like for about $6,500. Then you decide that your old push mower will work just fine anyway (after all it's your spouse that mows the lawn). As you walk away, you can start planning your next vacation because you just saved $6,500.

One more. This one's a little tougher. It'll take a lot more discipline. Wives don't let your husbands try this one alone. It will save you the most...but it can be very tricky to succeed at.

Go to your favorite tractor store (ours is green) and find one of their latest models, maybe even hook it up to an implement you are fond of. Depending on your salesman, you might even be able to demo it for a few hours. After you have smelled the new paint, played with all the new controls, and sat in the super luxurious seat—walk away and save a quarter of a million dollars.

This is where the wives are needed. I have found that sometimes the men's hands seem to clench so tight to the steering wheel, it becomes necessary to remove one finger at a time. Pliers are often needed. Pushing, dragging, pulling, and roping are all acceptable forms of force for the wife to use.

It's always tough to save that much money. Sometimes husbands don't find the savings to be worth it. So I recommend this saving venture only for the very dedicated. And never, ever try it alone—the success rate drops exponentially. Now, with these money-saving tips under your belt, I wish you long life, and pug-dog prosperity.

Say Your Pwayers, Wodent!

The plant disappeared into the ground as quickly as money is sucked into the pneumatic tube canisters at the bank. I knelt down quickly where the melon plant used to be—there was nothing but a few roots stuck on the side of a freshly-dug gopher hole.

My insides were screaming in my best Elmer Fudd impression. "Hewwo! Acme Pest Contwol? Weww I have a pest I want contwolled!"

If jumping up and down and waving around a gun would have helped Elmer, I may have been inclined to try it too. I stood in the middle of a gopher colony, surrounded by rodent-chewed drip tape fountains.

Yesterday it had been a beautiful field of freshly laid mulch with pretty little melon plants growing down the rows. Today, gopher mounds dotted the field like a traumatic case of teenage acne. And if the pimpled field wasn't enough, the rotten rodents had chewed the drip tape into fishnet stockings—holes spraying water every which direction. Some plants were drowning in water, some were bone dry, and others raptured—nothing left but a few roots to mark their life in this world.

"Eat my pwants and chew up my dwip tape will you, you wasically wodent?"

I wish there was something I could put in the water that wouldn't hurt the plants, but would repel those horrid-buck-toothed rodents. My aunt's vegan, black-bean brownies would do the trick—the first person to take the bite has their mouth glommed shut, and it repels everyone else—but I'm afraid they might kill the melon plants too.

I felt like the star of a cartoon. Chasing around a tiny little nemesis who is always getting the upper hand. The only thing missing was to be sprayed in the face with water from the chewed-up drip tape. About that time I knelt down to start working on another patch. As I put my hand on the plastic it sunk into a flooded gopher hole. Water didn't spray my face, but my knee, my boot, and my arm up to my elbow sunk in the mud. "Kill da Wodent!!" I breathed.

That evening, covered in mud and scratches, my husband and I headed for home. Neither of us spoke. It had been a long and discouraging day. Our cat purred for attention, and rubbed across our legs, but we weren't in the mood. We tossed him out before changing out of our mud-encrusted clothes and heading for the kitchen—each of us wishing we had a wife that had supper on the table when we came home. Too tired to cook, we just sat at the table staring dejectedly at each other.

Meow. Meeeeoooww. MEOW! The cat was demanding to come back in. Our cat, perhaps trying to cheer us up (but more likely to add insult to injury), was sitting at the door with a mouse in his mouth. Before I could shut the door on them, he ran into the kitchen and dropped it. The bewildered mouse took off running under my kitchen counters and disappeared.

"We are not a catch and release family!" I shouted to the cat. "Get him back, get him back!" The cat looked up and lazed off into the living room.

The next morning, with rodent traps set inside the house and in the field, I was not in the best of moods. That's when my son came running in the house. "Look at all my four-leaf clovers!" He opened up his hands to display dozens of the little green lucky leaves.

"Wow, that is a lot!" I exclaimed.

"Ya, I wasn't finding any, so I just glued an extra leaf onto the other ones."

Simple and profound. Those rodents may have gotten me yesterday...but staring at my son's four-leaf clovers, I felt my luck was just one bottle of elmer's glue away from changing.

"Be vewy vewy quiet, I'm about to go hunting wodents!"

The Farmhouse

My theory on housework is, if the item doesn't multiply, smell, catch fire or block the refrigerator door, let it be. No one else cares. Why should you?

~Erma Bombeck

Grandma's Ketchup Soup

I wasn't sure what I was expecting 17 years ago, when I went on my first date with my husband. Dinner and a movie maybe? Flowers or candy, maybe a peck on the cheek goodnight. What I did not expect was watching the Sound of Music—with his grandparents.

We drove to a tidy little blue and white house—tulips and roses lining the sidewalk.

Usually one has a little more time to prepare for "meeting the parents" or grandparents in this case—like several months, maybe a year?

As if first date jitters weren't stress enough, now I had to try to make a good impression on three people.

His grandmother was worrying too—albeit for different reasons. She was concerned about us sitting idle in front of the TV for *three* hours. We had hardly made introductions before we were hustled in to the back room, and given scissors and felts to cut out for a project she was working on.

For three hours we listened to Julie Andrews sing while we dutifully cut out felt animals and stacked them into piles.

The date while unusual, unorthodox, and *productive*—turned out to be enjoyable enough that one turned into two, then five, and before I knew it, his grandmother had invited me back for a birthday party.

The whole family turned out, a lovely dinner was set... then the guest of honor was pushed up to the head of the table...Niki, the family poodle. He had a nicely shaped can of dog food on a china plate, with carrots for candles. I guess the surprise showed on my face, because my boyfriend leaned over and whispered "at least this year she didn't make everyone's food look like dog food!"

Going to her house became an adventure—and you could never predict what was going to happen. But the door was always open—and she was always willing to set an extra plate.

One evening we dropped by at supper time. "Oh there's plenty of tomato soup," she said, scurrying to set 2 more bowls on the table.

"Here, to make sure, we'll just add some ketchup and water, after all it's mostly tomatoes anyway, right?" Ketchup soup?

Mmmm, can't imagine why the Campbell soup company hasn't picked that line up yet?

My husband's grandma, known to us know as "Great Grammy" loves to keep her hands busy (and anyone else's hands that seem idle for that matter). Age doesn't matter to her. If you have hands that are functioning, there must be something you can use them for. On a camping trip to Lehmann hotprings, in between riding 4-wheelers and soaking in her pretty, flowered bikini, she overheard two of the little girls complaining of being bored. Well, that is not a word anyone should use around Grammy. She quickly shooed the girls outside and had them making assembly line mud pies. I'm not sure who was having more fun—but boredom and idle hands were both gone.

On another family camping trip, she lost her Pampered

Chef can opener. She was sure it had gone into the trash. After searching the whole trailer, the rest of the family gave up and went hiking...but it was a valuable can opener, so she stayed behind and kept looking.

Arriving back into the camp site, we found Grammy at her organizational best—near the dumpster—with a small group of other campers (some she knew, some she didn't) and had convinced them to help her dig through the trash in hopes of finding her "very expensive" can opener.

It eventually did turn up—in a bag of bananas *in* the camp trailer. But I will never forget that little group of people digging through the dumpster—simply because Grammy had organized again.

A few years ago, she joined us for a 4-wheeler trip to the Oregon coast. She had been seeing a new male companion and spent the majority of our trip waving her cellphone around trying to find reception to call him. Many times throughout the day we would see her out on the beach standing on a big rock, her back to the wind and the phone pressed tightly to her ear.

One afternoon after finishing a fresh batch of hot, homemade salsa, she came into the camp trailer from one of these calls, a big grin on her face. She set her phone on the counter and with an expression of glee announced. "I have found myself a new lover!" Just for the record, hot salsa seems even hotter coming out your nose!

Great Grammy may have turned 90—but idleness is still not a word in her vocabulary. She may not be doing the same felt projects she was 17 years ago, but I dare say, that if my husband and I showed up on her doorstep, with the Sound of Music, she would be delighted at having three hours to keep our hands busy on one of her latest projects. I think we might give her a little extra warning though, so she won't have to stretch the ketchup soup quite as far.

Life is like a Box of Crayons

My grandma was an artist. An artist that loved colors. If I was to personify her life, I would have to say it was like a box of crayons. And not the little 8 pack...no, she's got all 96 colors. She wouldn't go for just red and blue and yellow. Her box would include atomic tangerine, blizzard blue and mango tango. And if I had to pick a crayon for her, she would have definitely been Razzmatazz—mostly red with a touch of jazzy pink.

Her crayon life taught me a lot. Some crayons are sharp, some dull. Others pretty, some have weird names, but each crayon can provide a story, a poem, or a life lesson. There may be some colors we prefer, but life is about using as many crayons as you have in your box.

Scarlet is the crayon that would describe some of the moments when Grandma would make Grandpa blush...one time in boarding academy, Grandma sparkled at Grandpa and said *"I love you great, I love you mighty; I love your pajamas right next to my nighty. Now don't get embarrassed and don't get red....I meant on the clothesline, and not in bed!"*

Grandma was so witty, she was quick with the retorts and often had a poem to recite as well. If she didn't have one, she'd write one. So when I see the Macaroni and Cheese crayon, the only thing I can think of is a poem she wrote a few years ago.

You can say stout or chubby, or pleasantly plump
too much size to the thighs, too much lump on the rump
too much jelly on the belly,
lacking thin 'neath the chin
doesn't matter how you quote it,
does no good to sugar coat it
the name of the game is the same
fat's fat, and that's that!

The crayon Screamin' Green made a routine trip to town memorable because Grandma saw a rattlesnake in the road, near their house. She drove over it...and then backed up and drove over it again. This was repeated in excess. Still not satisfied, she drove home, returned with a shovel and proceeded to chop off its head and bury it.

Grandma then used the snake as an illustration to Tammy about how we need to stay far away from evil things... because even when we think they are harmless (like the dead snake), they can still hurt us...just like a rattlesnake can poison even after he's dead. Grandma felt proud of herself for not missing a teaching moment, and asked Tammy if she understood.

Tammy nodded, "If I ever see a snake, I'll get you and not grandpa!"

Eggplant and squash aren't the same color...but they are often both lumped in the uneaten food category, so the eggplant crayon brings to mind my aunt Brenda's pancakes. Trying to be sneaky healthy, she filled the batter with squash.

Taking the plate of squashy pancakes to my Grandma, she says "Mom, I want you to tell me these are the best pancakes in the whole world." Grandma replied, "Honey, these are the best pancakes in the entire world."

"Mom, you have to eat them first."

Grandma smirked as she replied "I need to pray for them first." Then she bowed her head, "Lord, thank you for the best pancakes in the entire world."

The crayon pink symbolizes breast cancer awareness... of which our family has been very aware. Most days were good, but sometimes Grandma would get really frustrated with nurses, receptionists and doctors asking brightly "how are you today?"

Since my grandma didn't think they wanted to really know, she decided to come up with answers they really didn't want to hear. Such as "well the buzzards aren't circling yet!"

Grandma gave us a gift...she didn't leave us a box of 4 crayons, or even 8. She blessed her friends and family with the whole 96 pack plus the sharpener!

Without her, it sometimes seems we are coloring with only blues and grays— but every time we tell a funny story about her, or recite one of her poems, we are actually pulling out those colored memories, and someday we'll see those colors have painted a rainbow in our sky.

So if you are ever missing a loved one, pick up a Razzmatazz crayon and remember:

Goodbyes are not forever.
Goodbyes are not the end.
They simply mean we'll miss you.
Until we meet again!

My Bon Bon Life

"Boy what a life you have!" the woman remarked.

I put the cap back on the syringe, and stuck it into the pocket on my coveralls. "Yep," I replied, "I wouldn't trade it for anything."

The woman nodded her head, "I mean, really, you are lucky, because you have more time than most people do."

"More time?" I suddenly realized where she was going with this. "I thought we all had the same allotted 24 hours?"

"Oh you know what I mean," she said.

I raised an eyebrow.

"Well, you don't have to go to work," she said exasperatedly, "which gives you time that most people don't have. Time that allows you to do crafts and projects or just whatever you want to do. Most people don't have that you know."

I smiled a fake smile, "Well speaking of time, I need to get back to vaccinating these sheep."

"Ya, I need to get some stuff taken care too," she smiled. "After all, some of us have to work for a living!"

It was a beautiful day to work the animals. I kicked the

mud off my Muck boots as I climbed back over the rickety fence. I really should fix that thing, I mumbled to myself, good thing I have all the time in the world to do it.

So in all my free time—in between watching soaps and eating bon bons—I decided to write up a Bon Bon recipe for all the women in agriculture that "are really lucky" because they have "more time than most people do."

My Bon Bon Recipe

•Start with coffee. This is an important first step.

•Mix in something for breakfast, you can substitute coffee for this step if you choose.

•Brush your teeth...you can use coffee for this step as well. This is known as multi-tasking.

•The fuel filter on the tractor is back ordered, and the battery on the ATV is dead, so you pack hay to the animals by hand.

•Read the "To-Do" list you made last night and start on the first one.

•Before you complete the first item on your list, answer the phone to discover another tractor has broken down, and the closest part is 3 hours away.

•Drink another cup of coffee, it's going to be a long day (good thing farmers have more time than most people).

•Load up the kids, bring their schoolwork along—may as well get their reading done on the drive.

•6 hours later, part in hand, it's time to find some food for lunch.

•Gourmet, home-cooked, all natural sounds great...but everyone's stomachs are growling, and the "to-do" list hasn't even been started on. So gourmet soup out of a can works...and coffee.

•Finally ready to climb in the tractor, where you will disk and play flash cards with the kids—at least until it's too dark in the cab to see what 9x3 is.

- Upon arriving home, feed the animals, feed the kids, restart the washing machine (maybe if you're lucky you'll get it in the dryer this time).
- Make another "To-Do" list for tomorrow. Basically, just add a few more things to your existing list—as you never even checked off the first item. If you can, set your coffee pot for the next morning. A rancher friend once told me the reason she drinks so much coffee is because she's too poor to buy alcohol.
- Sit down to pay bills and hear a loud commotion outside. There are sheep prancing on the porch, which awakened the cats, which awakened the rooster, which awakened the hound—insert phone call—which has now awakened the neighbors.
- Drink coffee, sleep when you can, repeat every day. Slight variations may occur in different elevations, seasons, or the type of agriculture you find yourself in.

She was right about one thing though—I wouldn't know what to do with a 40-hour work week. Forget 9-5, farmers and ranchers prefer 5-life.

Shampoo & Horseshoes

It's the little things in life...

"How do you open this thing?" my husband asked, walking out of the bathroom holding a bottle of toilet bowl cleaner.

"Is it broken?" I asked, tilting my head to see the bottle better.

"I don't know, but it seems to be stuck," he said. Still trying to twist it as he headed for the kitchen junk drawer. "Are my pliers still in here?" he asked, pulling the drawer open.

"It's a new bottle," I said, "I can't believe it'd be broken."

I took the bottle out of his hands to look at it. I squeezed the lid and turned—and it opened right up. I gave my husband that one eyebrow look.

"Well how was I supposed to know you had to squeeze it first?"

"Guess that means I know how many times you have scrubbed the toilets in our house, then, huh?" I teased him.

He gave me a pretend glare, "I just prefer to use AJAX when I clean them."

I rolled my eyes. "And to think, it is women who get a bad rap for not being able to open their own jars and bottles. First it was the shampoo bottle and now toilet bowl cleaner?"

I smiled, and the years rolled back in my mind's eye.

My husband and I had just started dating, and he had invited me to come stay the weekend at his parent's house. His mom was quite hospitable: we had a delicious supper of baked potatoes with a cold cucumber sauce, and then she pointed me in the direction of my bedroom and handed me a towel and washcloth.

The next morning, I showered, then went upstairs to help with breakfast. I had just finished setting the table when my boyfriend walked up the stairs, "Did you use the shampoo that was in the shower?" he asked.

"Ya, " I answered. "Why?"

"There was shampoo in the pump dispenser."

While I was showering, I had reached down to pump some shampoo in my hand. The dispenser was locked but the bottle was half-empty. I unlocked the pump, squirted some in my hand—and then, thinking that maybe he was one of those super particular kind of guys, I squeezed it back down and locked it.

"Well?" he asked.

"What? Was I not supposed to use that shampoo?"

"It was there to use, I just want to know how you made the pump dispenser work."

"I unlocked it, and then—"

"It unlocks?" he interrupted.

He groaned, "You're remembering that stupid shampoo dispenser, aren't you?"

I smirked. The little things often become big things

over time. My grandma used to recite:
> *For the want of a nail the shoe was lost,*
> *For the want of a shoe the horse was lost,*
> *For the want of a horse the rider was lost,*
> *For the want of a rider the battle was lost,*
> *For the want of a battle the kingdom was lost,*
> *And all for the want of a horseshoe-nail.*

It wasn't a war—but a pesky bottle cap did cause me to lose out on having someone else clean the bathroom. It's the little things for sure!

The Procrastination Tree

The early bird may get the worm...but it's the second mouse that gets the cheese. A motto I have often repeated to myself when I seem to be getting behind—with life.

Just last week while fixing breakfast, I looked up at the Christmas tree that has tormented my psyche all year. Last January it begged to stay up a little longer. In February it joked that at least its ornaments and ribbon were red. It made green St. Paddy's jokes in March, and asked for Easter ornaments in April.

Thankfully by May it was time to be back in the seat of my tractor and I didn't have to look at it anymore. Occasionally during the summer, I would glance up in the loft and see the Christmas tree branches drooping farther and farther down. Many times I thought "tomorrow I might have some extra time to take it down."

Funny thing about tomorrow though. Although it is a noun—it's really a mystical place where 99% of all human production, motivation and achievement are stored—and you need the correct "open sesame" password to get in.

October arrived, and I am pretty sure I could hear that

Christmas tree snort with laughter as I packed in two pumpkins for jack-o-lanterns.

"Hey, these decorations are different!" I shouted to the tree in my head. Regrettably, the tree was right. The pumpkins are still on my porch...uncarved. "It's just been a busy year!" my inner dialogue justified to the accusing Christmas tree.

Every time I walked through the kitchen, I could feel the procrastination jokes falling like needles from the dead and brittle Christmas tree.

"You say procrastination, I say ingenious avoidance...either way, you aren't coming down til later...I'm too busy," I'd retort to the tree in my imaginary guilt exchange.

"It's November..." the tree gloated. "You usually put up a tree the day after Thanksgiving. What are you going to do this year? Have a changing of the guard...er...tree?"

"I'm taking care of my procrastination issues...just you wait!" I'd threaten back. And the tree would only laugh...in my mind...in my sleep...in my dreams. Have you ever had so much to do you became overwhelmed? I've learned at those moments, you can just lay down on the floor—for a really long time—and if anyone disturbs you, call it meditating!

Suddenly, it was December...and I still had last year's tree up—fully decorated. Which wouldn't have been entirely bad—if it hadn't been a live tree. Although in all honesty, I don't think it had been alive for a really long time.

A fresh Christmas tree was cut and stood up in the living room. I packed the boxes of Christmas decorations up from the basement and felt a wave of guilt as I walked under the loft where the dead tree still sported his star.

"I'll get to you next!" I thought.

"Right!" he chortled, "I've heard that for nearly a year now...Procrastinator!!"

"I don't procrastinate, I just put it off till the last second because then I'll be older and therefore wiser, and can do the job better!" I defended myself senselessly against the insults the guilt in my own mind attributed to the dead tree.

One morning, my husband and I were planning our Christmas party. One of the games we were playing required the participants to decorate a Christmas tree despite the many hurdles and challenges we were planning to throw at them. Like losing their Christmas tree.

Only one team, we had decided, would actually get a real tree to decorate, one group would have a wooden pallet tree, and another group would have a DIY tree—a tall smooth log, a pile of loose pine branches—and a drill. But we were still one challenge short—or we were until I glanced up into the loft. Suddenly my procrastination had found a purpose!

During the party, one of the ladies came up and complimented me on such organization and planning. I smiled and was just starting to thank her, when she continued, "I mean, to have the foresight to keep last year's Christmas tree? That is real planning!"

I walked over to the dead tree, now decorated in plastic Easter eggs and paper ribbon, "Ya hear that Killjoy? Foresight and planning!"

The tree, made one last crack at my procrastination, but with my guilt gone, I barely could hear him. I put the Pro in procrastination, and looked around the party, I must say I will no longer feel bad about keeping my current tree up through Valentines.

The Story of Your Dash

The two dates on a tombstone take longer to carve and seem to provide the most information—but it is that small dash between the two that really tells the stories.

When we pause to walk down memory lane, it is rarely the birth and death dates we remember, but the laughter, the embarrassment, the frustration—in essence, that small dash of memories.

We recently laid my uncle John to rest, and the memories from his dash were no different...we laughed, we grimaced, we cried...and we repeated some of the phrases and idioms that made up his life. My uncle always had a silly or sarcastic quip to life. Even if they weren't said aloud, his facial expressions were often idiom enough.

One December when my uncle and my dad were just kids, they decided waiting until Christmas to find out what was in their beautifully wrapped packages was just too difficult. They carefully unwrapped all of their packages. After they had looked at their soon-to-be gifts, they carefully rewrapped them and put them back under the tree with none the wiser. I'll bet their letter to Santa that year could have started: *"Dear Santa...I'm so GOOD at being naughty....Which list does that put me on?"*

There's a fine line between fishing and just standing on the shore like an idiot. But that line doesn't have to be connected to a fancy pole to catch fish, as my uncle learned early in life. On fishing trips his dad would break branches, peel them a bit, tie on some line, hand them out to the boys and point them in directions far away from where he wanted to fish. Perhaps it was the fact that their dad had a real pole and they didn't, or maybe it was just a real love of fishing. The boys, however, always seemed to manage to bring back fish to their surprised father.

My uncle and his brothers grew up on motorcycles and they never stopped riding. The last time he and my dad rode together was on 4-wheelers. After riding a few hours, my dad noticed he was alone. He found my uncle—on foot and the 4-wheeler about 50 feet off the trail, on its side, with sagebrush poking out at all angles. My uncle grunted "the 4-wheeler wouldn't stay on the trail." My dad felt it was most likely the loose nut behind the wheel giving the machine fits. *When life throws you a curve, lean into it...but try to keep it on the trail.*

I've heard it said that if you *teach your child to love motorcycles, they'll never have money for drugs*...but I guess that isn't always the case. One family story is told about a time when John bought some drugs from his brother. Then, he wrote a sign advertising his wares for sale...at school. Needless to say his pharmaceutical career wasn't off to the best start. It's funny each brother tells a bit different version of that story...but one way or another, thankfully...each of the two brothers discovered better ways to make money...ones that didn't involve talking to the "nice officers."

We learned one of my uncle's favorite phrases years ago while working in the melon sheds. I don't remember exactly what was asked the first time, but his response was "it not my yob." You wanna unload that truck "it not my yob." You wanna sweep the floor? "it not my yob." He said it so much it became practically synonymous with his name. He was the only person at the melon sheds that had a forklift certificate and could pick quarters up on the forklift forks with ease. But all those things are filed secondary in my memory...just after "it not my yob."

John also really enjoyed yard-saling. Finding treasures was exciting to him...He was the first person I heard use the vernacular "dumpster diving." And while I am not sure he ever actually dove in a dumpster, he did enjoy his stint working at the landfill...he was constantly talking about the great treasures he had found and brought home. We may have teased him about it, but no one was making fun when his yard-saling bought us kids a giant trampoline.

I can see my uncle saying that only dead fish go with the flow, because you were never 100 percent sure what he was going to do next. One time, while visiting his brother, he walked into the kitchen where his niece was eating breakfast...and perhaps because the bowl was the right shape, or just because the mood was right, he decided she needed a milk facial. And before a good morning could be exchanged, her nose was touching the bottom of her cereal bowl.

My uncle also really enjoyed participating in the church's Journey to Bethlehem event. He was the most excited camel dung salesperson I've ever seen...okay so he's the only camel dung salesperson I've ever seen....but I can't imagine that any Bible era camel dung salesperson could have mustered up as much enthusiasm as my uncle had. Another year he was a beggar...and again, got into the part so much that people walking through the event actually even tried to give him money!

Five years ago he was diagnosed with an inoperable brain tumor. I know people say a leopard can't change its spots but while lying in that hospital bed, he made a fist and said he was going to fight. That maybe it was his "yob" after all. Unfortunately, it was a battle he couldn't win. And a closing date was added to his birthdate...but memory is a way to hold on to the things we love, the things we are, the things we never want to lose—in essence, one's dash. As we trade our 24 hours for 1 day of memories, ask yourself: How do you want people to remember your dash?

The Year of Biscuits

I hummed as I took down last year's calendar and put up a new one. Earth needs a speed limit. Its trips around the sun move at an alarming rate—and each year it seems to be accelerating. Maybe a speeding ticket or two would slow it down to a more manageable pace. Making New Year's resolutions a little easier to attain? I look at my last year's goals scribbled in pen on January 1:

• Lose those 10 extra pregnancy pounds. Hey look at that, I only have 13 pounds to go to check that off my list! But I can't be too critical, after all, it takes talent to cram a 14-day diet into 2 hours and 21 minutes. I did discover a pretty awesome new workout though. It's like a cross between a lunge and a crunch—I like to call it lunch!

•Make cardio a priority. Pretty sure I took care of the entire year of cardio that afternoon I discovered a spider crawling across my neck. Cardio, kickboxing, I'm sure there was even some karate thrown in there for good measure. No one liked that little end table anyway.

I didn't bother writing new resolutions on the calendar

as I tacked it on the wall. Instead, in block letters across the top of January it reads: If you want to reach your goals...you must shrink the size of your "but."

After adjusting the new calendar on the wall, I thumbed through the old one. Last year was not my favorite. I said some things I regret—I wish I could go back—I have since come up with much wittier insults and retorts. I did some things I regret—like forgetting the linens in the washing machine for nearly a week! Seriously though, it was a tough year. A year of death. A year of readjusting and change. And change, as we all know, can be very painful.

Makes me think of a story set in a small southern church. One Sunday morning, the pastor called on one of his older deacons to lead in the opening prayer. The deacon stood up, bowed his head and said, "Lord, I hate buttermilk." The pastor opened one eye. "Lord I hate lard." The pastor was perplexed. The deacon continued, "Lord, I ain't too crazy about plain flour. But after you mix 'em all together and bake 'em in a hot oven, I just love biscuits. Lord, help us to realize when life gets hard—when things come up that we don't like—that we need to wait and see what You are making. After it's all through mixing and baking it'll probably be something even better than biscuits. Amen"

I looked back at my old calendar. I hate buttermilk...but when I looked past the days to the individual moments, I could almost smell the homemade biscuits.

There was laughter and snow flurries while building snowmen. Enjoying a midnight snack with my husband after checking ewes during lambing season. Taking my 7-year-old to see his first Star Trek movie in the theater. Snuggles on the couch with cocoa while my son reads me his favorite story—*The Titanic*. Those moments my husband slips in behind me, and we silently watch our two boys sleeping. Those were my moments of biscuits.

I made no resolutions this new year—but I am going to

try to shift my thinking from buttermilk—to biscuits. Start thinking about all the excitement the new year will bring—last year I called it stress—but this is the year of biscuits! I tossed the old calendar in the trash.

Light a few candles, burn a few bridges, and buckle your seat belt for another dizzyingly fast spin around the sun.

Well that Didn't go as Planned

*B*ad decisions make great stories...and this was a whopper. I kneeled over our bathtub, pulling pieces of epoxy paint out of the clogged drain. Years ago, when my husband and I were first married, our bathroom sported a colorful collection of Pepto-*dismal* pink fixtures and sea foam green tile and floor.

One day while he was on a hay run to the other side of the state, I installed a new white toilet, setting the old pink one on the lawn to greet my husband upon his return. Later, while he was again hauling hay, I enlisted my mom's support and we sent the pink sink to ugly appliance heaven. The big, pink cast iron tub however, seemed a little bit more daunting. I stood in the hardware store admiring the sleek, white fiberglass ones, knowing they were well out of my realm of expertise. How to get the old one out seemed the most problematic—my husband would love to help with house repairs—if they were "income-generating projects." Unfortunately, I haven't been too successful with installing a "pay bathroom."

Then I saw it. On the end of the bathtubs display I found a box of epoxy paint for toilets, sinks and bathtubs. I picked it up. I felt my tub dilemma slipping away under a lovely coat of white paint.

"Don't do it." A voice behind me said.

I turned to see a general contractor friend of ours. He warned me that I wouldn't be happy with the end results for long, as he had never seen one that lasted more than a few years. I listened, and my brain heard, "It'll last a few years... and then perhaps you will have had time to figure out how to encourage your husband to help you install a new one."

A half-baked idea is okay...as long as it's still cooking in the oven. But I pulled that idea right out and bought it. Within days I had a lovely white tub—which lasted almost a year. Then came the "peel and plug" stage which left us with the only thing uglier than a pepto-bismal tub—a pepto bismal tub with a little milk of magnesia thrown in! It was a great example of a bad idea.

My mind contains many good ideas...but sometimes brain forgets to tell me which is which when it squeezes them out. My 1-year old enjoys sitting in front of steering wheels pretending to drive. He'll pull the key out, and put it back in, push and pull every light and button, until the windshield wipers are going crazy, the hazard lights are flashing and the radio is blaring some horrible station.

One evening while waiting to load a hay truck, he was playing in the front seat of my Jeep. In the dark, with the top down, I could imagine the keys being thrown outside and lost into the sea of goat heads. I figured they would be safer with me. The risk I took was calculated—but boy I must be bad at math! My Jeep sat in that same location for nearly 2 weeks before we finally found the keys—the keys that I had so carefully taken away so the baby didn't lose them.

You are always one decision away from a different life. It's amazing how even the smallest of decisions can change your life. When my oldest son was learning how to talk, he said "Daddee" for almost a year before he said "Momma." I told my husband it was my turn this time to be first. And you know? The worse you want something the worse you get it. I said every variation of Mommy imaginable to my littlest son. And then one day he said it "maMA." I clapped in delight, he'd said Momma before Daddy. He pointed at his thermos then at me and said "maMA." It was a beautiful moment. Then he pointed at his snacks, and later his toys, each time saying the glorious word "maMA." That was in the morning.

By that evening it was "maMA, maMA," getting louder each time if he thought I didn't jump fast enough.

By the end of the week, he was relishing his own personal assistant and I was begging him to say "Daddy." They say everything happens for a reason...but sometimes that reason is that you are stupid and make bad decisions.

Wreck the Halls

To the top of the tree! To the back of the hall....Now dash away! Dash away! Dash away all! And did they ever dash—with me chasing right behind! We had been scurrying around that morning, getting ready for my littlest to have his baby dedication at church. I had bought him the cutest little knickers and bow tie with a matching newsboy hat—and he hated it. He pulled off the suspenders, kept throwing the hat, and twisted his bow tie just as quickly as I could get it in place.

My curling iron kept timing off, and each time I was about ready to use it, the baby required more attention. I finally gave up on curls—and just twisted my hair up in its usual wad—curls are overrated. Finally, both boys were dressed, the pickup was warming up—and that's when it happened. CRASH. My beautiful 13 foot Christmas tree was laying in a heap of shattered ornaments while two cats hopped around it still hissing and spatting at each other. My baby started to cry. My 7 year old pointed like Tattoo on Fantasy Island as he jumped shouting "Ze Tree, Ze Tree!"

I took off chasing the offending cats out of the room and down the stairs. I could almost hear their smug little cat voices singing "Oh Christmas Tree, Oh Christmas Tree....Your ornaments are history!" Suddenly, I had insight into one of the characters in my favorite childhood nursery rhyme: Three Blind Mice. That poor Farmer's Wife had just had enough—they caught her at a bad moment and she just happened to be using that carving knife. My cats should be glad they were born without tails and that all I wielded was a baby newsboy hat!

We pushed the tree back up, but it had tipped in the stand and was leaning haphazardly into the room. Not wanting to be late for church, we just pushed it into the corner and left it—broken ornaments, torn garland and all.

All was fine—until the next day. The doorknob on our front door decided to stick. We tried and tried, but it was not going to open. After several minutes of standing in the cold with a baby who had already kicked off his shoes and pulled off his socks. We made the decision to go in the back door—the one in the corner where the tree was propped up. We tried to squeeze in without disturbing the disheveled tree—but it was not to be—the tree crashed a second time, breaking the few ornaments that had escaped the "cat"astrophe.

We stood it back up a second time—but I just couldn't bear to look at the cursed thing. After another day in the house, it went back to the tree lot. (Lucky for me we sell Christmas trees, or I doubt I could have exchanged it. As it was, my husband still grumbled about having to haul multiple trees in and out of the house—before Christmas. He said this was not the kind of tree lot where you get to take the trees for a "test drive").

Finally a second tree was put up—this time with shatterproof ornaments. And the cats are officially on the naughty list. Instead of raindrops on roses and whiskers on kittens, bright copper kettles and warm woolen mittens, the cats are getting their least favorite things: new flea collars, cat shampoo and water spritzers. My kids are learning a valuable lesson from this though. Don't mess with the Farmer's Wife! Especially at Christmas time—she may not get your tail—but your gift of a new Lego set might morph into a bathroom cleaning kit before you can say Three Blind Mice!

I am So Thankful

Like many Thanksgiving meals before it, we spent 4 hours shopping for the menu, 6 hours chopping, cooking, braising and blanching, and within 20 minutes all that was left of the gorgeous spread of holiday delicacies, were a few photos on memory cards. The food was delicious, and I began making a mental checklist of things I am thankful for.

1. I am so thankful that while I don't enjoy cooking, I was blessed with a family that does...and does it well.

I looked around the leftovers, waiting for everyone to finish seconds (and thirds), so we could move on to the pie table. 14 different pies stood tempting: everything from huckleberry/jellymelon to peanut butter pie. Some nearly works of art. My mouth was watering. I looked down at my stomach, which was protesting the idea of more food, even those delectable desserts.

2. I am so thankful for elastic waistbands...it makes gluttony so much easier to attain.

Soon the games came out, and I quickly found myself in a somewhat violent game of Nerts. Cards were flying across the room, occasionally accompanied by vegetarian cursing. We played quite a few rounds, each time putting me farther in the hole.

3. I am thankful my Grandpa taught me to be such a good loser. I mean, not that I really lost, because it was really just a friendly game...and if I would have really wanted to, I could have cleaned their clocks...if I would have wanted to.

We had just finished up another round that I'd let my siblings win, when I got an unexpected phone call. One of our sheep, who were still on "summer pasture," was lambing. We quickly left the game I could have won, and started the drive back home. Leaving the delightful smells of dinner and the family bickering that comes with Thanksgiving, to round up my sheep...in the dark.

4. I am thankful for neighbors that go the extra mile to help out. One neighbor let us use his trailer, drove it to the field for us, and both he and his wife helped to load them... all in the dark...and without corrals.

By the time we arrived at the field, the new mom had two healthy lambs on the ground. We got them in the trailer, but we weren't quite as successful with the rest of the herd. We would almost have them—and then one would double back, and they'd all be gone.

5. I am thankful for bummer lambs...without bummers we wouldn't have caught any of them.

After a few attempts, we loaded what we'd caught and called it a night. The next morning we went back for the rest of the herd. The neighbor again met us with his trailer. There were two more baby lambs dancing around the pasture.

6. I'm so thankful for healthy lambs and ewes that have good maternal instincts.

In daylight, the sheep weren't so spooky, and it wasn't long before they were loaded up and heading home. I was exhausted. Running on a Thanksgiving stomach is hard work. To recap: we spend 4 hours shopping for our meal, 6 hours preparing it, and the next week working it off.

7. I'm so very thankful, that Thanksgiving only comes once a year!

Laundry Fund

It was laundry day, and no matter how carefully I checked, it seemed I missed hidden trinkets and treasures in each load. Some of them, no worse for wear, got dropped into a little John Deere treasure bowl. And the others—the ones that melted as effortlessly as on the Wicked Witch of the West just got dropped in the trash.

    I was really bummed to see I'd washed one of my favorite $85 hair clips. I don't typically go for the trendy new looks and styles...but I do spend a little more when it comes to hair clips. My husband doesn't seem to mind though. Each clip comes with a free hotel stay, a complimentary breakfast, and usually a pool and hot tub. The clips come in all colors and have many logos on them. Some of my favorites say Best Western and La Quinta. They're perfect, I can pull my hair back with them and they double as a writing utensil. The downside to your hair fasteners being full of ink is that sometimes they go through the wash...like now. My nicest set of sheets now had big ugly black ink spots all down one side. I started to feel sick...until I decided just to make the bed up with the ink on my husband's side. IF he even noticed, he'd probably assume he'd stained them with greasy jeans. He wouldn't want to bring it to my attention, and I wouldn't have to see the spots. Win-win.

Later that evening at the farmer's market, the subject of laundry came up. And we began talking about the treasures we have found in the washer and dryer. One woman said she confiscates anything that comes through the laundry—it becomes her tip for washing. She said over the course of a year, she was able to collect enough money to take her family on a nice vacation. We were all laughing and agreeing what a great idea it was. I'm sure we were all thinking of ways to implement the idea into our own homes—ideas of vacations dancing in our heads.

That night, as I put my last load of laundry into the dryer, I noticed that John Deere treasure bowl sitting on the shelf. I couldn't remember the last time I looked inside it. I scooped it up, set the laundry basket down, and plopped down on the stairs to count up our new vacation fund.

I found 6 dollars and 27 cents, 3 Canadian pennies, a tarnished bracelet, a broken brooch, a 5/16 socket, 4 bolts, 5 nuts, 2 lock washers, a grease zirc, a broken drill bit, an unclaimed key, an empty tube of chapstick, a sprinkler nozzle tip, and 2 unidentified objects. So unless those unidentified objects score me a place on the Antiques Roadshow, I think my dreams of Paris are out...although I might make an afternoon matinee...if I go alone and skip the popcorn. At this rate my new fund won't even cover my damaged sheets!

Alzheimer Clutter

*H*ell hath no fury like a kid catching you throwing something out...even if it's a broken toy or a torn coloring page. Trying to toss broken crayons makes me feel like a drug smuggler, keeping away from the watchful eyes of my 5-year-old cop.

I hate to admit it, but I can relate to his sense of attachment. Some of it is sentimentality (I can't throw away that ugly sweater that I've never worn because my dad got that for me when I was 17), and some of it is practicality (as soon as I throw something out I will find a use for it...now with Pinterest, I'm almost afraid of throwing away old buttons or wrapping paper tubes...I may need them someday.)

And so I continue to grow my "collection" of random trinkets, scraps of wood, rocks, paper, ribbons, pretty cards, ticket stubs and other tidbits that I've treasured over the years.

This Holiday season I was starting to feel that tug of conscience that says I really need to trim down and throw out. That thought was fluttering in my head while I was looking for a particular scrap of ribbon for a Christmas project. It wasn't in the first drawer I looked in, nor the second. I had to stop a moment and think of where I may have put it.

My eyes scanned my craft room: taking in boxes and drawers and shelves cluttered with my project materials. I opened my fall decoration box. I pulled out the glittery red ribbon and stared at its sparkles for a moment.

I've heard people say that doctors recommend crossword puzzles and other brain games like sudoku to stimulate the memory and prevent Alzheimers. I looked around my craft room again. This time with different eyes. Dozens of boxes, as many shelves and quite a few drawers—all holding hundreds of small items.

It was an exercise in memory (and sometimes agility) to find any of those objects. I smiled. A big, happy smile of relief. Not only would I not have to part with any of my treasures (I mentally throw a fit just like my 5-year-old when I throw stuff out), but I can justify keeping them as an Alzheimer deterrent. No more mind-squeezing crosswords either—I'll just do more crafts and projects!

I was still smiling happily to myself, when I ran out to the shop for a drill bit to help complete my project. I opened first one drawer than another in the toolbox. I found the drill bit case, but it was only half full and I wasn't lucky enough for it have the size I needed. 20 minutes later I still hadn't found it, and I was starting to get grumpy with my husband. He has several perfectly nice and mostly empty toolboxes while his tools are scattered all over the shop.

I finally found the pesky bit just as I was about to blow my top. I snatched it up and was stomping back to the house...when I realized...my husband was just practicing Alzheimer prevention too. My anger quickly dissipated, we're both taking steps to ensure a ripe, memorable old age.

Mommy Milk Cow

I milked my first cow at my grandparents house when I was little. So little, I had a hard time balancing on the little 'T'-shaped milking stool, and my fingers didn't seem to reach all the way around the teat. Finally my grandma sat on the wooden stool, and pulled me in front of her. She wrapped her own hands around my fingers and "we" milked the cow together. Filling up the bucket with warm frothy milk, while every once in a while "shooting" a stream into the cat's tin.

Since then, my milking experience has covered sheep, goats, and dogs (don't ask). Mostly recently, with the addition of a new baby, I have experienced life on the other side of the fence, as my family has begun affectionately (I hope) calling me Mommy Milk Cow.

Within days of giving birth, I came down with mastitis, and soon learned that "feeding on demand" has much less to do with the baby's demand than the mother's. As I was trying (often unsuccessfully) to fill up the baby's walnut-sized stomach with a grapefruit-sized quantity of milk, I realized that it was from sore, tired, engorged, nursing women that coined some of the most common "Mom-isms."

1."Don't play with your food!"

Said the sleep deprived mom who just wants her baby to eat, so she can go back to bed

2."You will stay there until all your food is gone!"

Said the engorged mom who came into her milk too suddenly and is dying from the pressure.

3. Think of all those starving children in (insert country of your choice) that would be delighted to eat your food.

Said the mom who is part Holstein and is swarming in milk enough to feed twins.

4. It's no use crying over spilt milk

Said the mom who accidentally sprayed her crying baby in the face with milk.

5. You just ate an hour ago!

Said the mom whose baby prefers little snacks around the clock instead of fewer more hearty meals.

6. You will eat it...and you will like it!

Said the no-nonsense mom who has already been through this 4 times before.

As the baby and I go through the above steps, in no particular order, I am starting to think I should get 2 henna tattoos across my chest, giving the baby the option between "Take It" or "Leave It."

As the Mommy/Baby dance will continue as he grows, I look forward to seeing what other phrases or words of wisdom I will start to view in a different light. But until then, I'll enjoy my role as Mommy Milk Cow...as long as my husband continues in his role as Daddy Diaper.

Tooth Fairies

*B*eware of half truths...you never know when that other half is going to show up. Mine showed up 3 weeks ago, and is still taunting me from a mug in my microwave.

The lie was pretty innocent. Actually, I'm not even sure that we thought of it as a lie or half truth. We told our son, (probably what most parents have since the age of the toothbrush), that if you don't brush you teeth, they will fall out. With the fear of gingivitis ingrained into our son, teeth brushing only needs gentle reminders such as "cavities" and "Grandpa's dentures," to keep his toothbrush well pasted.

And all was well. That is until 3 weeks ago. He came up to me at the farmer's market, pale and shaking. He looked terrified and he wouldn't talk. It took much prompting before he whispered "I've been brushing, I really have!" It took my mind a minute to shift gears from watermelon sales to teeth brushing. I sat on the edge of the trailer as he leaned against me.

"I know you have, Sweetie," I tried to soothe him. "So what's the matter?"

"My tooth is wiggly. And I really have been brushing."

Oh boy. I tried (most unsuccessfully) to convince him that it was normal to lose baby teeth. But all he could think about was rotten teeth and his great-grandpa's dentures. I was thankful when one of his older friends came up to play. As they walked away I heard her telling him about the teeth she had lost.

When we got home that night, he was in slightly better spirits, but still pretty terrified of that wiggly tooth. He never played with it, wiggled it, or tried to pull it out like I remember doing with my loose teeth. Over the next few weeks the tooth kept tilting farther and farther out, and there were days I wanted to just yank it out.

He still thought that somehow it was his fault for not brushing. We read a couple of stories about kids losing teeth, but nothing seemed to help, he just kept reminding us that we were the ones who told him why teeth fall out. Finally his tooth fell completely forward. I told him stories about my first loose tooth. It had no more started to wiggle, than my dad, impatient in his desire to become a toothfairy, had taken pliers and pulled it out.

Horror crossed my son's face as he asked "Really? Really? Did Papa really do that?" Oh yes he did. My husband told of pulling his first loose tooth with a string and a door. At this point, I fear our son thought us nuts. He practically bolted out of our room.

Half an hour later he reappeared, a trickle of blood around down his lips and his hand held out as far as he could reach. "I pulled it out," he gasped. I tried to give him a hug, but he shook free as he kept pressing the little white tooth my direction. "Take it!" he pleaded. I can stomach many things.... but teeth are not one of them. I quickly pushed him into the kitchen. So thankful that the toothfairy from my house never collected teeth from under pillows. Instead, my family toothfairy preferred teeth in a mug of water in the kitchen windowsill. He happily emptied it out of his hand, as it splashed into the water and started to sink I wondered if my parent's hated the idea of touching teeth too?

Thankfully, I'd not have to touch it. Just dump out the tooth, replace it with change and fill it back up with water... or so I thought until my husband came in. "How can you throw out our son's first tooth?"

"Um, what am I supposed to do with it? I already took a picture."

"My Grandma saved her kids' teeth and hair!" He insisted as he took the cup out of my hand. His eyebrows furrowed as he looked at the little tooth sitting on the bottom of the mug. "I don't know. Maybe we can just hide it in the microwave, until we decide."

I gave a great sigh, as I pulled out a matching mug and dropped in quarters and water to put back in the windowsill. The next morning as my son collected his dollar out of this cup, and told us that he knew we had put the money there because the tooth fairy wasn't real, I was wishing we hadn't been so truthful about that. Because every kid who believes in the toothfairy knows they only leave money IF they can take the tooth....and I knew his tooth sat in another identical mug just inside the microwave door.

I'm afraid my half truth will haunt me...at least until I give up on the truth about what really happened to that tooth. It may make me a liar—but I am not my husband's Grandma!

Tupperware and Socks

Getting ready for the upcoming holidays, and friends and festivities has prompted our annual fall closet cleaning. And with each cupboard and shelf that is cleaned out, I am both pleased and puzzled. Pleased because it always feels good to minimize, puzzled because I never am quite sure how all the junk got there in the first place. Those two feelings followed me throughout the house.

In the living room there were books I've never seen, written by authors I don't read; magazines I don't subscribe to, nor have ever bought; and a few ugly knick-knacks I don't remember collecting. In the bedroom I found a box in the back of the closet filled with unmated socks. Why did I keep them? I have no idea. Why they ended up in a box in my closet? Just as good a question, with just as bad an answer. I have no idea.

The closet was filled with clothes that no longer fit anyone, shoes no one wore even when they were new, and sheets that fit a bed we haven't had in 3 years.

It was easy to fill a garbage can in the bathroom. Half empty (or often completely empty) bottles of hair and skin care products lined the shelves in the cupboard. Why do we keep these things? Or put them back in the cupboard? I asked myself this over and over as I tied my second bag of trash.

The kitchen was no less full of random things we didn't need. I found spices I don't know how to use, boxes of crackers no one has ever liked, and home-canned jars filled with "goodies" I can't identify—in jars that are not mine. Under the sink I found more almost empty bottles of dish soap and cleanser and other cleaning supplies. Is there some kind of subconscious thing that prevents us from using something all up before opening a new bottle?

I kept going through the cupboards, dishes I didn't know where came from, spoons that didn't match any utensils I own, even a tablecloth I've never seen before was tucked away in the back of a drawer. I must say though, that even though each cupboard brought its own puzzlement over the contents, I was still feeling mighty pleased with myself for all I'd accomplished. The living room was full of boxes marked Goodwill, Basement, Junk and one marked Husband...just because I figured he should at least double check his junk before I tossed it. The last cupboard in the kitchen I went through was home to all my Ziploc, Tupperware, and Rubbermaid containers.

By the time I was done, I had found a couple of dishes without lids, but I had a whole stack of lids without dishes. How does one end up with so many extra lids...especially since I seem to clean them out every few years?

My first reaction was to make a neat stack and put them back in (on the off chance I found them later), but then I remember my husband's advice about putting things in the fridge just to let them "finish dying." Still not quite able to just toss them in the trash, I put them in a box and hauled them out to the Junk pile in the living room. I'd let my husband haul them out, then I wouldn't feel quite so bad about tossing perfectly good lids. I set it right next to the box of single socks.

Chatting with my mom later about these oddities she laughed, "I am pretty sure that unmated socks die and come back as mismatched Tupperware lids."

From now on, I will have a less difficult time throwing away unmatched socks and lids...as long as I toss them out together I can think of it less as "junking" them, and more like reuniting lost loves.

Detrimming the Tree

Being the middle of February, I decided it was probably time to take down the Christmas tree. Everyone's always so anxious to put it up, but when it's time to take it down, I seem to find myself alone. I'd been hinting around for the past few weeks that it needed to come down, in hopes that someone would volunteer to help—with about as much luck as a pink leprechaun.

I'm constantly hearing moms complain they never have time to themselves. Some even spend extra minutes behind the bathroom door just because they find some alone time. Maybe it's different in other people's houses, but in mine, all I have to do is say "That Christmas tree is looking a little dry...maybe we should take it down..." and suddenly everyone remembers long-forgotten items on their to-do list, and within seconds I am standing alone looking at a dead Christmas tree.

This year was only marginally different...the baby didn't know what a to-do list was. And so the two of us sat on the floor, alone in the house, and stared at the brown, decaying remains of Christmas 2015. As much as I Samantha'd my nose, the tree still hadn't disappeared, so I set the baby down, and began hauling up the empty ornament boxes from the basement. I set the boxes in front of the huge, dead tree, and I wished I was rich enough that I could push the whole tree—decorations and all—out the door, and just replace it all next Christmas.

I got a few ornaments carefully put away, before the baby started fussing for attention. Soon, my years of careful organization went up baby cries. I looked around at the upset baby and the empty house—and since no one else was there to criticize, I just started pulling things off the tree, and dropping them in the nearest box or sack. The ribbons and garland I began yanking out, and the candy canes I may as well eat.

The tree shifted this way and that, and soon the tree stand was spinning on the hardwood floor. The baby began waving his hands in delight at the dancing Christmas tree. More ornaments, random boxes, and I didn't even care. So what if they are a little bruised next year? Everyone loved the Velveteen Rabbit—and he was the epitome of bruised. The baby's happy cries made the unconventional tree detrimming continue.

I gave another strand of garland a good jerk to untangle it from the stiff branches, and sent a shower of needles onto the rug. It was still stuck. More tugs, more pulling and it seemed I had more needles on the floor than on the tree. I wasn't worried though, if a dancing tree will make the baby laugh, a smoking vacuum cleaner would be just as entertaining.

The living room was about at its worst: ornaments ripped off the tree, garland in piles, and the plastic from a candy cane wrapper stuck to my cheek—when our elderly neighbors dropped by. I would have been embarrassed, but about that time the baby reminded me the tree was no longer dancing, and he was bored. She took in the scene—looking like the "nightmare" on 34th Street—and graciously volunteered to hold the baby so I could go back to my mess.

When I was done, her husband helped me haul it outside. We mashed, shoved, pried and pushed to get the brittle tree through my door and out onto the lawn. I was about to haul it to the burn pile...until I remembered a story my grandmother had told me about a friend who always left her mop bucket out after the floors were done—just to make sure her husband knew how hard she had worked that day. I dropped my end of the tree right then and there.

Usually the Christmas tree just disappears one day, along with all the ornaments, and no one seems to ask or wonder what happened to it. It's just one of those things that happens—like clean, mated socks magically appearing in your drawer. If I left the dead tree on the sidewalk, maybe it will be noticed, and maybe, just maybe, when my husband moves it, he'll think about all the hard work that went into taking down the tree, and I'll get help next year.

When he came home later that day, I watched as he came up the walk...and went around the tree, barely even glancing at it. The tree stayed on the sidewalk several days before the wind blew it off and into a tree..and there it is still sitting.

I guess dead Christmas trees are cousins of the empty toilet paper roll—men just can't see either one.

Diaper Duty with Dad

Two percent snakes, snails and puppy-dog tails, and 98% breast-milk, all bundled together in a little thing we call a diaper. The last few years our house has seen only a slightly elevated testosterone level, being that our 6-year-old will usually take my side. Yet, with the addition of another little boy, the tables have turned...and suddenly I have become the mom of boys. No longer is flatulence disturbing, and poop has suddenly become a source of laughter. Several times I have caught both my son and my husband standing over the baby and cheering him on. How did this suddenly become cool?

Diapers have also made changes to our family (no pun intended). I used to think of changing a diaper much like opening a gift from my Great Aunt Gertrude, you never knew what you were going to get...but you were pretty sure you weren't going to like it. But my 6-year-old finds Diaper Duty with Dad to be a fun and highly entertaining portion of his day.

With the first gurgle of the baby's intestines, my 6-year-old goes running for Dad, "Daddy, you have to change a diaper!!" he shouts gleefully. Then he awaits as eagerly as a kid at Christmas to see "what kind of surprise Daddy gets!"

Diaper changes around here have become a melodramatic climax of our days. My husband and son make faces, noises, and all manner of wiggly antics while changing the baby's diaper. After the 'event' is over, my son likes to tell me in great detail what kind of "surprises" Daddy got, along with his reaction to each one. My son then waits anxiously for the next one, questioning every so often "Diaper Time yet?"

I knew diapers have been a constant thought in my son's brain since the little baby has arrived, what I didn't know, was how much my husband had been thinking about them too.

Have you ever noticed the intense thoughts that cartoons seem to have? We've all seen as Donald Duck's eyes spin like a slot machine before a pie comes slowly to a stop where his pupils used to be. It's the same with Scooby Doo and sandwiches, Monterrey Jack with cheese, and Wile E Coyote with the Road Runner. I know the look well...my husband has one too. He sees life in dollar signs. It doesn't matter if it's income, or outgo, he follows money as closely as a cash register. This is not an obsession, he just thinks in dollars... it's just the way he is wired.

We will be baling hay, I see the sun glinting on the tractor and mentally capture the deep red hues of the day's end burning into the bales and reflecting the baler's cloud of dust. My husband? He's looking at the sun hitting the tractor and calculating how much longer we can bale before the moisture starts cutting into our profit margin. He's looking at the baler and thinking about the cost of replacing one of the knotters. He's also thinking about how much each bale actually costs. He will have the operator, wear and tear on the tractor, twine, grease, and shear bolts all figured in.

I have always known about his odd quirk...I just didn't realize quite how extensive it was...until I overheard a conversation he was having with my dad.

"Boy, babies are expensive!" he exclaimed. "Did you know that each diaper change can cost me up to a dollar?"

He had calculated the cost per diaper, the amount of Desitin used, the price per wipe, and the laundry that is often involved. He considered that sometimes the clean diaper gets soaked before it is fully fastened, and the next one often only lasts a few minutes before filling up, so one diaper change could involve 3 clean diapers.

It happens sometimes, even in the best of families...a baby is born. But that's not necessarily a cause for alarm. The important thing is to keep your wits about you, and buy stock in Pampers.

How to Care for your Mums

*A*fter a long groundhog winter, it is finally spring...or is it? It's a season of dressing in layers as Mother Nature plays April Fool's pranks the entire month: warm, no cold; sunny, no rainy; calm day, no thunderstorms. Summer's warmth is felt in the sun, and winter's icy fingers in the shade. No need to get overly excited when the first day of spring arrives though...as the first spring day may not come for nearly another month! But with May day and Mother's day right around the corner I thought it appropriate if we touched on a little "Mum" care.

The first thing to do is determine if you have an indoor or an outdoor "Mum." The indoor variety don't like the bugs, animals, rodents, or unpredictable weather. The outdoor variety of mums don't like areas congested with other plants.

Once you have determined what kind of "Mum" you have, the next part is proper care. Some people plop the mums into a pretty pot without taking them out of their black garden center pot. Your mums will last longer if you take the time to re-pot them. They need a pot with adequate room for their roots to grow.

Outdoor mums also need space. They don't thrive well in areas where they have to compete with other roots. Keep them at least 18 inches apart. They say love grows best in little houses, but having enough storage to put away the ever growing collection of toys and shoes and towels is really essential for the health and well-being of the "mum."

The potting soil should also have decent drainage. It is important that the water doesn't build up and mold the roots. Keeping the soil drained is as easy as saying grace, saying "I'm sorry," saying "I Love You," giving second chances, and giving hugs. Well-drained soil is a good way of keeping the mum well-watered and healthy.

Next, make sure your mums are getting enough sunlight. Mums love the sun. Make sure indoor "mums" have clean windows to get the best sunlight. For outdoor "mums," a tropical beach has pretty nice sun. If a trip to find sun around the equator isn't in your budget, a picnic, an afternoon at the river or a few hours in the hammock is a good way for your "mum" to soak up some much-needed vitamin D.

Make sure to give your mums water. Don't just pour water over the top of them and let it drip down into the soil. That's just asking for the mums to develop fungi and perhaps a bad mood. Instead, water close to the roots of the plant, saturating the soil. Kind words, genuine compliments, pictures children have painstakingly scribbled with broken crayons all go straight to the heart of the plant. If you notice their leaves starting to wilt, they need to be watered more frequently. Maybe a nice refreshing bubble bath will hydrate Mum again.

Lastly don't forget to "deadhead" your mums as necessary. Use your fingers to pinch off any dead flowers or leaves. Try to cut them off about the next set of leaves on the stem. When life happens as it so often does, don't let your "mum" keep those dead blossoms as reminders. Let bygones be bygones, let go of the past. Deadheading helps make your mums look neater and prettier, and helps to extend how long they bloom.

Different varieties of mums grow and flower at different rates. But all in all, they are pretty easy to care for. They are delicate, yet not too fragile to handle a little pinching and pruning. And they give more than they take in the time they require. The bottom line is that mums are wonderful for your home...indoors or out.

The Crisper:
Where Good Intentions Go to Die

*F*inding something to eat at our house usually goes something like this:

Open fridge. Nothing.

Open pantry. Nothing.

Lower standards and repeat.

I've often wondered how the fridge can be so full and yet have so little to eat. That is, until last week. My husband and I were cleaning up after dinner, and I put the leftovers in containers and Ziploc bags. "Um, really?" my husband asked, picking up a Ziploc bag filled with green beans. "Did you think they were worth saving?"

"Well, I'll come up with something," I shrugged.

"Did you like the beans?" he asked.

"Not really, but they weren't bad."

"Weren't bad?" He hiccuped. "The texture was horrible, the flavor was worse and they were stringy. What part wasn't bad?"

"I don't know, maybe I can make a casserole or something out of them," I answered, still focused on cleaning up from dinner.

"Do you want to eat them tomorrow?" he asked, walking away from the fridge still holding the bag of green beans.

"Well, not really, but I'm sure I can come up with something."

"What about the next day? You want to make something out of them for the weekend?"

I looked up from wiping off the counters. He was standing over the garbage can with the bag of offending beans.

"What are you doing?" I gasped, scurrying around the island, intending to take them from his hands and put them in the security of the crisper.

"Well?" he questioned, holding the bag out of my reach. "Do you want to eat them this weekend?"

"Not really, but there's nothing really wrong with them." I protested.

"So the way I see it," he says "is we can throw them away now, or I can put them in the fridge, and wait for them to finish dying and you can throw them out then."

I stopped reaching for the beans. "Well, when you put it like that...." I mumbled.

He dropped the bag into the trash, and proceeded in opening the fridge door for me. Dish after dish of past meals were stacked high. Some edible, some in the same category as the beans, and then there was the crisper.

Cucumbers slowly disintegrating in the back of the drawer, celery that made wimpy look strong, salad tinged in brown leaves, and sad, shriveled little carrots—it was like the nursing home for food. I burst into giggles. I had this sudden desire to print a sticker to go on my fridge drawers that would read: "The crisper: where good intentions go to die."

My husband continued to razz me about my "good intentions" that I save too long, and how much more food we would eat out of the fridge if I would use a little discretion before the leftovers went in.

"If I was the one in charge of putting food away, we'd have a much emptier fridge," he teased.

I was laughing at myself too, until I noticed a kitchen canister sitting out from the wall. I pushed it back until 'clank,' it hit on something glass. Upon moving the canister, I choked on my own laughter.

There was the cup of water with my son's tooth in it. After sitting in my microwave too long, my husband said he would take care of it. Now here it was, hidden behind my flour.

I held up the glass and in as straight of face I could muster I asked "So, should we throw this out now? Or put it in the fridge until..."

I Fought the Lawn... and the Weeds Won

I stood back and looked at the pretty burgundy flower pots sitting on my deck—filled and overflowing with nearly-dead flowers. How is it that I always seem to choose the plants without the will to live?

While the mornings were still chilly and frosty, I planted my greenhouse full of watermelon plants, garden plants and some flowers for color. The plants grew, the frost took a summer sabbatical, and we all got ready for the hot season.

My husband is happy to help with the garden—as long as he can do it from the seat of a tractor. Which meant that he rototilled and our boys helped transplant the trays of plants—or as the local rodent population refers to it—*the all you can eat buffet.*

We *planted* cucumbers, tomatoes, herbs, and all manner of pepper plants—we *grew* morning glory, kochia, squash and puncture vine. Have you ever noticed how squash and puncture vines never fail to reach maturity? You can spray them with acid, beat them with shovels, even burn them under a propane torch—and they seem to love every minute of it!

Gardening requires a lot of water—most of it in the form of perspiration—which may be why mine looks like a lovely patch of goatheads with small, almost indiscernible rows of produce. The recipe in the garden seemed to be Seeds + Water + Sun + Dirt = Weeds. However, while weeds dominated my garden, I was pleased with my flowers pots full of lovely annuals and perennials planted around the house—at least initially. Then they too began to show their true colors—and I don't mean with beautiful blossoms.

"What's the difference between an annual and a perennial?" my oldest son asked.

"Well an annual dies every year...and...a perennial? They die as soon as they leave the greenhouse."

As the summer wore on, the temperatures rose, my flowers drooped—and the weeds thrived.

I've read that plants react to people's voices, and that soothing words make them grow better and healthier. Don't believe it. I pulled weeds. I yelled at the weeds. I called the weeds mean names and hit them on the head. I scolded them in my gruffest voice—and they multiplied almost as fast as the rabbits eating my garden.

When it comes to weeding, some people have advised the best way to make sure you are removing a weed and not a valuable plant is to pull on it. If it comes out of the ground easily, it was a valuable plant. While there is definitely truth to that, I think that a better way to tell is to pull them both up—whatever grows back is the weed. But be warned: give the weeds an inch and they'll quickly take your yard!

Rock gardens might probably be a better choice for my green thumb—then again, the person that owned our property before us must not have had good luck with them either. I think the rocks must have all died, because he sure buried an awful lot of them. This whole area seems to be a rock cemetery!

Recently I was talking with one of my dad's high school classmates. She lives in Arizona and was visiting Oregon to attend their high school reunion. She was telling us about the beautiful azure pots that sit on her deck.

"How can you keep them alive in such hot weather, especially when you are traveling so much?" I asked her. Thinking about my own plants that seemed to dry up between between breakfast and supper.

"It's Arizona—plants get *'dehydrated'* so quickly that it's best to buy beautiful pots and plant them with fake flowers!"

Dehydration! That's it! I didn't have "dead" plants in the pots on my deck...they were only dehydrated. All they need is a little IV (imitation vegetation) and they'll look as good as real..er I mean new!

I imagined my flower pots filled with beautiful fake flowers. I'm afraid though, that fake plants would probably die too because I'd forget to pretend to water them.

As I look around the lovely patch of kochia, goat heads and rows of dehydrated flowers that we affectionately call home, I decided what I grow best in the garden is tired.

Weeds, dehydration, and fake flowers—if only people concentrated on the really important things in life, there'd be a shortage of life jackets, and an overstock of shovels, pots, and silk flowers.